Perfect Wedding Planning

Cherry Chappell is an independent public relations practitioner and writer. Trained originally as a journalist, she regularly reverts to type, writing features for national newspapers and magazines. During her career, she has organised many events, large and small, and for three years was co-organiser of the annual *Woman's Own* Children of Courage Awards at Westminster Abbey. Cherry is the author of two books: *Minding Your Own Business: Survival Strategies for Starting Up on Your Own*, 2004 and *How to Write Better Letters*, 2006.

Other titles in the *Perfect* series

Perfect
Wedding Planning

Cherry Chappell

BOOKS

Published by Random House Books 2008

8 10 9 7

First published in the United Kingdom in 2008 by
Random House Books

Random House Books
Random House, 20 Vauxhall Bridge Road,
London SW1V 2SA

www.rbooks.co.uk

Addresses for companies within The Random House Group Limited can be found at:
www.randomhouse.co.uk/offices.htm

The Random House Group Limited Reg. No. 954009

A CIP catalogue record for this book
is available from the British Library

ISBN 9781905211104

Penguin Random House is committed to a sustainable future for our business, our readers and our planet. This book is made from Forest Stewardship Council® certified paper.

Typeset by Palimpsest Book Production Limited, Grangemouth, Stirlingshire

Printed and bound in Great Britain by Clays Ltd, St Ives plc

Contents

To the couples who shared their experiences in this book. And to those now planning their weddings. May they all flourish and be happy ever after.

Acknowledgements

This book could not have been written without the marvellous and hugely generous help of the following people. I thank them all very much.

Donald Adams; Holly Andrew, Pall Mall Stationers; Rosie Ames, Green Union; Daljit Bhurji; Julia Boggio, Julia Boggio Photography; Esther Boyd; Adrian Bradley, Home Office Press Office; Suzanne Brown, Cornwall Registration Service; The Revd Guy Bridgewater; Terri Chandler; Peter Craft, Secretary, National Association of Toastmasters; Andrew Cussens, Bloomsbury Films; Jamie Cotter-Craig, Triggerfish PR; Elizabeth Fox; Val Gilfillan, The Association of Registration and Celebratory Services; The Revd Christobel Hargraves; Pasquale Lamanno, Foreign & Commonwealth Office Press Office; Chrissie Harten, The Gardener; Mustafa Jaffer, The Hussaini Islamic Centre, Stanmore; Taki Jaffer, Portsmouth Interfaith Forum; Paul Mackley, Perfect Day Cars; Mrs Ummulbanin Merali; Gino and Mike Meriano, Pink Weddings; Richard Clark-Monks; Ben Morris, the Church of England Press Office; Laura Morris; Rupert Morris; Ann Outram and Lindsay Gill, Healthspan; Sebastian Pole, Pukka Herbs; Terry Prendergast, Marriage Care; John Rabey, John Rabey Solicitors, Truro; Rev. Dr Raj Sharma, The Hindu Priest Association; Patrick Swan; The Revd Canon Celia Thomson; Christa Valsin, C'est Deux.

Introduction

More than just an event

One of the most delightful weddings I have ever attended – and there have been quite a few over the years – was that of Esther Morland and Howard Boyd, both committed Quakers. There was no set service, no music, no flowing white frock and no bridesmaids. Instead, there was a warm and considered declaration by Howard and then by Esther in front of their family and friends who packed the Meeting House at Street, in Somerset. Guests then, as they felt so moved, stood and perhaps read from the Bible or spoke about their wishes for the couple. On leaving, we all signed the Quaker certificate of marriage. It was an entirely happy event and was memorable because of its integrity and simplicity.

So, let's start by considering what a wedding is meant to be. It is a very special rite of passage for two people, marking a significant new stage in their relationship. They are making a formal and public declaration of their commitment to each other and their intention to embark on a new life together. It should therefore be a highly personal celebration. In the majority of cases it will take the form of an exchange of vows at a ceremony, possibly of religious significance, before family and friends. Usually some form of festive meal or party will follow.

It sounds simple enough, but for many people this event holds all kinds of worries and preoccupations over and above the mechanical aspects of organising a 'do'. Families in the 21st century are complex groupings with strict hierarchies and differing allegiances. Family pride and position within a community may come into play, which may impinge on the wishes of any couple wanting to 'keep it simple'. Sometimes a couple will come from different cultures or from different faiths, or they may be a same sex couple, or a much older pairing. This may mean that they have to accommodate the concerns of others around them as well as making their own preparations and adjustments to married life.

The organiser therefore has to cope with not only the practicalities but also the highly charged emotions surrounding the event, and must balance the wishes of the couple themselves with the expectations of their family and friends, while making it a memorable and fun occasion for everyone.

This guide considers how to structure both parts of the event (the ceremony and the reception), create the budget, set a style and ensure that everyone understands the part they are going to play, looking at how to co-ordinate all the necessary practical requirements and assistance. It shows how it is possible to make the event a positive memory for everyone involved, considering how to cope with multicultural and multigenerational concerns, courtesies and sensitivities, avoiding family clashes, and it shows how to deal with the unscheduled – what to do when things go wrong.

This book deals with a largely Western (or Westernised) concept of the wedding, be it religious or a civil ceremony. However, we also look at some other traditions, which have many fascinating and meaningful aspects that readers may wish to consider – and perhaps integrate – when they are making their wedding plans. We also look at alternatives to the highly expensive and glitzy wedding by considering how to add style and special meaning without spending a fortune, and ways to make your wedding ethical and green.

Making Magic

Organising a large family celebration, with all the necessary attention to detail, is a complex affair and therefore a major undertaking. Amid the lists and inevitable pressures, it is worth remembering at regular intervals what the event is for. It is to provide the marrying pair with a joyous day that they will look back on with pleasure for the rest of their lives. It should set the tone for the years to come.

All the very best events have a dusting of magic to them. In a tough old world, we all need a little enchantment. However, this is not something that can be ordered up, bought and paid for. All you can do is create the atmosphere in which the magic can occur. It is the personal touches that will give the occasion true meaning: a particular piece of music, wearing the jewellery that belonged to a grandmother or special friend, the loving messages from people unable to attend, the declarations and speeches that reflect genuine feeling and family pride, the bridegroom playing the drums at the reception party. It is from such elements as these that abiding memories are made.

Imagination and consideration, along with warmth, love and humour at every stage of the planning are the good precursors to the creation of a truly special and *magical* event.

Cherry Chappell
Chelsea, 2007

1 First steps

So it's a happy match. It's all agreed between the couple, and maybe between the families too. A wedding *will* take place!

Among the first decisions are:

- deciding whether it will be a religious or civil ceremony
- setting the date
- deciding a budget -- this in itself may set the size and tone of the event
- creating the 'shape' for the event.

One of the initial steps, however, is to decide who will organise this marvellous occasion.

Who is the lead organiser?

Home Planners

The majority of weddings are still organised from home, usually that of the bride. There is a lot to do, so it is possible that having a small team of helpers would be useful. Whether it is one person or several, someone has to take the lead. In many instances, this is the bride's mother. Where there is an older bride, or the mother is absent or unable to undertake this role, it may be the bride herself who is the main organiser. Sometimes a stepmother, sister or aunt will step in.

If there is likely to be a clash of ideas – or wills – it is better that both parties discuss the likelihood of dissension at the outset, and take the grown-up decision to remain calm and sensitive to everyone's concerns. A wedding should be a special day for the bride and bridegroom, not a family battleground. However, major celebrations of this kind are also a meeting of the clans and often family pride asserts itself!

If one family member is likely to try to dominate, it may be worth deciding a specific role for that person, or even firmly explaining that they will not be expected to take a major part in the arrangements. You could say: 'We know how busy you always are and we feel that it would be an imposition to ask you to do too much, and there is much that we would like to do for ourselves. However, we would like to feel we can ask for your advice!'

If the bride and groom are from different cultures or faiths, it may be both appropriate and courteous to ask the bridegroom's family to share in the planning. This way, misunderstandings may be averted, and new ideas for celebrating both cultures can be brought in to play.

The professionals

As we become materially richer but increasingly time poor, it is not surprising that so many brides are turning to professional planners. At the time of writing, some sources suggest that up to a quarter of weddings are now organised by professional wedding organisers.

There are many adverts for wedding planners in glossy brides' magazines, but if you decide to have some help, it is worth investing time in finding the right planner for you, one to whom you can relate and fully trust to help you design your perfect wedding day.

The benefits of professional planners is that they will already be familiar with all the opportunities and options, and can help you to develop the style of wedding you seek within your specified budget. They will be able to show you a range of local venues, as well as know where to find all the other necessities, from catering to hairdressing and limousine companies to photography. If you wish, they will set up the arrangements for all of these services, and look after many of the fiddly details for you. It's wise to set up an initial consultation with at least two different planners to establish what sort of service each provides. The initial meeting is also important to ensure that you have complete trust in your planner to act on your behalf. After all, you will be working closely with them over a number of months. It's important that you like them.

The best route is always personal recommendation, but if that is not forthcoming, it is worth looking at the umbrella organisation, the UK Alliance of Professional Wedding Planners. This organisation requires high standards of its members, and has training schemes for people coming into the business. It has a directory on its website (www.ukawp.com), which shows accredited members in various parts of the country.

If your proposed planner does not belong to the UKAWP, it's important to check that the company has:

- a good track record, with a portfolio of weddings to show you
- references on offer
- public liability insurance.

It is also worth asking if the planners receive commission from suppliers such as venue and catering companies, and, if so, whether they pass the commission on to you. Some planners ask for a fixed fee; others take a relatively small fee, but take the commissions to make up the difference. Check if there will be any extra charges for the planners such as their travel, accommodation and administration. Be quite sure you know who is paying whom and for what.

There are planners who offer a specific service to help you organise a wedding in an exotic location abroad. Many of these can be found via the internet. If you would like a wedding in Monte Carlo or Hawaii, you simply put 'Monte Carlo weddings' or 'Hawaiian weddings' into the search engine and up pop the web addresses of the appropriate companies. Wedding planning outside the UK may be unregulated, so unless you have a personal recommendation, ask for references, and be prepared to check them. We look further at weddings abroad in Chapter 9.

There are some companies that specialise in civil partnerships, and we discuss gay weddings in Chapter 6.

The best planners will be working on your behalf right up to and including the day. Even so, the professionals can only offer their experience in arranging the event. They cannot decide the guest list – or choose the all-important frock. Someone has to make the decisions on behalf of the bride and bridegroom. If you decide to select a planner, ensure that you have a contract with them that clearly lays down what the responsibilities are on both sides. Keep close contact with your planner and be sure to tell him or her as soon as possible about any developments or changes you wish to make.

What kind of wedding ceremony?

If you have decided to marry abroad, you may wish to skip this section and go straight on to Chapter 9.

If however you are marrying in the UK, the next major decision is whether you will have

- a religious service (other than the Church of England and Church in Wales, you will require a separate civil service first or a registrar to be in attendance)
- a civil ceremony on its own
- a civil ceremony followed by a service of blessing
- a civil ceremony followed by a humanist ceremony.

The latter three may suit same sex couples entering a civil partnership or those where the partners are coming from different faiths or hold non-religious beliefs.

Remarriage

Different faiths and churches hold differing views about the marriage of people who are divorced where their previous partners are still living. However, in the Christian tradition, it will be the decision of the individual minister as to whether to arrange a remarriage or a blessing ceremony.

Who are the key players?

Once you've decided on the sort of ceremony you would like, you can start fitting the other elements in to place, and I would recommend giving thought to the key players in the wedding early on in the process. It's no good having the perfect venue if your nearest and dearest can't be there with you on the day.

The bridal party

In Christian and many civil ceremonies, couples still opt for the traditional bridal party. Although it is not obligatory, many brides prefer to be escorted down the aisle by their father, step-father, brother or close family friend. Some still wish to be 'given away' although the significance of this – the transfer of a woman from her father's to her bridegroom's care (or in olden days, property) – has less meaning.

Bride's attendants

Many brides from many different faiths still like to have attendants: bridesmaids (if single) or matrons of honour (if married) and pageboys. Originally, in the Christian tradition the group, duly veiled, was meant to act as camouflage for the bride, so naughty spirits would be confused and not whisk her away. There's less whisking too nowadays but, in practical terms, it is quite useful to have someone to help arrange long frock, train and veil and headdress, deal with unexpected presents, and keep track of the flowers and so on. Younger family members usually thoroughly enjoy the honour, although very small children may become tired and fractious with all the strangeness and excitement.

The chief bridesmaid may also help organise the hen party and help the bride get ready on the day, as well as being in charge of the younger attendants. She usually holds the bride's bouquet during the ceremony.

Best man

The best man has an important and extensive role to play. He will often organise the stag party and help with the arrangements for the reception. He will usually be the main contact for the verger (at a church wedding) and be in charge of the ushers. This means he will need to know about anyone who has special seating arrangements or requires special facilities, such as someone in a wheelchair, or the photographer and videographer. He will also check that the order-of-service sheets are being distributed by one of the ushers.

He will escort the bridegroom to the ceremony, preferably arriving at least 20 minutes before the bride is due, and he will retain all necessary documentation. Much beloved of comedy shows, it is also his task to keep the wedding rings safe and produce them at the required point during the ceremony. After the service, the best man will often help the photographer gather together guests for group shots, before ensuring that all the guests have left for the reception with any necessary directions on reaching the venue.

At the reception he will organise the receiving line if there is no toastmaster and, at the appropriate time before or more usually after the meal, announce the speeches. He will make the third speech, during which he will thank the bridesmaids and read out any cards, emails or telephone messages (see Chapter 19), and will then announce the cutting of the cake. If a dance follows, it is his privilege to dance with the chief bridesmaid.

If the bridal pair are leaving immediately for a honeymoon, the best man will often be invaluable in arranging for the cases, transport and travel documents to be available at the scheduled time.

Ushers

The ushers' role is to assist guests arriving for the service. This may mean directing them to car parking and helping anyone who is elderly or disabled. They will hand out order-of-service sheets and hymn books and escort people to their seats. The usual form is that the bride's family and friends sit on the left hand side facing the altar, the bridegroom's on the right. Latecomers are normally directed to sit at the rear, and parents with small babies may also wish to sit close to a door. It is also useful if the ushers have access to umbrellas and one fully charged mobile phone (which of course will be silenced once the bride has arrived). By the way, there's no reason why the ushers have to be male; it's quite in order to have female relatives or friends in this role.

The minister

If you are having a religious service, your next port of call should be the minister. Most faiths have a form of preparation which they prefer couples to undertake before their marriage.

Ministers of the Church of England or Church in Wales are all able to perform the marriage service without the involvement of the super-intendent registrar. People from all other Christian denominations and from all other faiths are required to have a civil registry service, followed by the religious wedding blessing, or a religious ceremony at which the registrar is present. The exception to this is where the religious building in which the ceremony will be held has its own 'authorised person' who can register the marriage, in which case a registrar need not attend.

The registrar

You can choose to marry or form a civil partnership in any registry office or at any approved venue within England and Wales. The registry office will have a list of those venues within your locality, but many others are available nationwide. These venues are discussed further on page 10. There are similar arrangements in Northern Ireland and Scotland but the procedures, documentation and time requirements, as you will see later in this chapter, are different.

Where will the wedding ceremony be held?

Once you've got your bridesmaids and best men lined up, it's time to start thinking about the venue.

Getting married in a church

In the Anglican Church (Church of England and Church in Wales) there is currently a residency requirement. The country is divided into parishes and the residency requirement entitles you to marry in your local church.

If you have a particular long-standing attachment to a school or college chapel or cathedral, you should discuss this with your local vicar first. In England, for instance, you can apply to the Faculty Office for the Archbishop of Canterbury's special licence. A special licence is not granted automatically and you should discuss the application with the minister who is going to conduct the ceremony. You can apply for a special licence up to 18 months in advance of the wedding date.

There have been recent changes in the Church of England making it easier for couples to marry in a church that has special meaning for them. The changes dispense with the former residency requirement. The new regulations must be approved by Parliament and receive royal assent and, if granted, will then take effect from autumn 2008. Of course you will still be entitled to marry in your local parish church, but couples may also choose to get married in:

- the parish where they were baptised and/or confirmed
- a parish they have lived in for six months or more at any time in their lives
- a parish in which they have attended worship for at least six months
- the parish in which their parents lived or worshipped during the child's lifetime
- the parish their parents or grandparents were married in.

You may be required to furnish proof of the connection, and you should discuss this with the vicar of your chosen church first. If you cannot meet any of the qualifying requirements, you may still be able to apply for a special licence. For advice, contact: www.facultyoffice.org.uk.

If your wedding will be in your local parish church, there is a legal requirement for banns to be read in church on three Sundays during a three-month period prior to the wedding. Under the new regulations, if you have chosen another church, the banns will be read in both your local parish church and the church in which you will be married. Christian churches prefer not to celebrate a marriage during the period of Lent, although some Church of England and non-conformist ministers will now agree to this.

Common licence

In order to marry in an Anglican church, it is also possible to apply for a Common Licence where:

- the marriage is between two foreigners, or a foreigner and a British subject
- one partner is resident in Great Britain but does not have British nationality
- one partner has British nationality but does not live in the UK
- the couple are living temporarily in a parish where they wish the marriage to take place
- the couple is no longer resident in England or Wales.

The residency requirement of a minimum of 15 consecutive days within the parish still holds, and the licence is issued at the discretion of the Diocesan Bishop. At least one of the partners must have been baptised. Again, consult the local vicar for advice on how to apply for this kind of licence.

Whatever the venue, remember to check the seating capacity. This will help you decide how many people you can invite to the ceremony.

Getting married in a registry office

You can make a provisional booking with the registry office's diary manager up to a year in advance. Most registry offices have several rooms. One will be a small room for a couple and the required two witnesses only, which may be appropriate if you are having a religious service or blessing afterwards. Then there will be at least one larger room available at a higher fee to allow for bigger parties, where music and readings can be given as well. When making a booking, it would be advisable to check the registry office's policy on confetti – some will allow biodegradable confetti – and on photography, sound recording and/or making a video at the proceedings. Usually you will be able to provide your own flowers, if you wish to do so.

Getting married in an approved venue

Bookings for approved premises may incur a booking fee. A registrar will attend your wedding at any of the approved premises in their area, the only limitation being that the service must be between 8 a.m. and 6 p.m. It is advisable to make a booking of both date and time for the registrar to attend the ceremony as soon as you have decided on your venue, since availability of registrars may be limited during busy periods.

You will also be advised at the time of booking about the necessary formalities. The first requirement is a formal notice of your intention to marry. Your local registry office will help you with information and forms. Some registry offices run an appointments system, since you must give the notice in person and you will be required to show original documents proving your age, marital status, address and nationality. This usually means your birth certificate, passport, identity card or Home Office Travel Document. If you have been married before, you will need to produce a Decree Absolute of Divorce or Civil Partnership Dissolution. If you have been married before and your partner has died, you will need to show both your marriage certificate and the death certificate.

If both the bride and bridegroom are EU citizens, the formal notice of your intention to marry must be given to the superintendent registrar of the district in which you live. If you live in different districts, separate notices will need to be given on each. If one or both partners are non-EU citizens, you must apply for special permission for your wedding and when it is received, you can give the formal notice of your intention to marry. These formal notices must be displayed at the registry office for 15 days before the authorities for your marriage can be issued.

We look at the shaping of the ceremony in the chapter on non-religious weddings on page 47.

When will the wedding take place?

You'll find that the availability of your key players and of your chosen venue will dictate the date your wedding will take place. You should be prepared for a certain amount of toing and froing as you find a time that suits everyone – holidays and work have a habit of getting in the way. But if you persevere you're sure to find a date that fits.

Many couples wish for their weddings to be held on a Saturday, so that the maximum number of guests can attend. If you have to avoid major holiday times and perhaps even much-loved sporting events as well, this leaves only a restricted number of Saturdays during the year. It's best then to establish a date as quickly as possible.

Not all traditions favour Saturdays. Those from the Asian traditions often opt for a midweek day. It is probably best to consider several dates and check that all those who will form the main wedding party are available before choosing the final date.

Marriage in Northern Ireland and Scotland

The procedures are not dissimilar in many ways, but it is worth being aware of the differences.

In both Scotland and Northern Ireland, religious ceremonies can only be solemnised by a minister, priest or pastor who is entitled to do so under their respective Marriage Acts. If you wish for a religious service or blessing, your first port of call should therefore be the minister.

Civil ceremonies can be held either in the registry office or an approved venue. There is a also a system in both Scotland and Northern Ireland where temporary approval can be extended to hold the civil ceremony in any venue of your choice, including your own home. For advice on how to make an application, contact the registrar of the district in which the marriage will take place.

Whatever kind of wedding you choose, you will be required to complete a Marriage Notice Form and provide the required documentation. Once the registrar is satisfied that there is no legal impediment to the marriage, a Marriage Schedule is prepared. Without this document, no marriage can take place.

For more information, the General Register Office in Northern Ireland has an excellent and easy to follow website: www.groni.gov.uk with a link to 'How to get married', as does the General Register Office for Scotland at www.gro-scotland.gov.uk.

2 Thinking ahead

Save the date

Having set the date, and checked with those who will form the main bridal party, you may wish to let other close friends and relatives know as soon as possible so they can reserve it in their diaries, even if some of the full details and the reception arrangements are yet to be made. This is a particularly good idea where guests have busy schedules or are likely to travel long distances and may need, for instance, to reserve flights. A good way to do this is by sending out a 'save the date' card. These have become increasingly popular and many stationers have examples.

Example 1

Please save the date of the wedding of
Jamie and Carole
Saturday 10th November 2007 in Lausanne, Switzerland

Invitation to follow
For more information please access the website
www.jamieandcarole.com

Example 2

Bernard Donoghue and Nigel Campbell
invite you to save the date of

Saturday 2nd June 2007
to join them to celebrate their civil partnership
at the Museum of Garden History
Lambeth Palace Road, SE1 7LB
Invitations will be sent in the New Year

Courtesy of Holly Andrew, Pall Mall Stationers

Next steps

While you are contacting the minister or the registrar you will also be able to check the elements that will make up your wedding service. Whatever kind of wedding it is, the chances are you will need to think about the following things:

- the marriage preparation expected
- the form of the service
- suggestions for readings and music
- any protocol and any fees relating to:
  - bells (Christian weddings)
  - music
  - permission for videoing the service
  - photography inside and outside the church
  - the verger
  - decorating the venue with flowers and garlands
  - the use of confetti
  - car parking and disabled access
  - rehearsals.

All these elements are discussed in more detail in later chapters.

Teamwork

Bringing the team of best man, bridesmaids – or at least the chief bridesmaid – and ushers together with the bride and bridegroom at an early stage is a good planning strategy. Deciding what is required and who is responsible for each task will save hours of phone calls, emails and panics nearer the time. The same team should assemble for the rehearsal, so they can be at ease and confident on the day itself. It makes for a much smoother-running occasion.

Hotel reservations

There is a rule of thumb amongst wedding planners that the reception venue should never be more than 20 minutes away from the service. It also makes sense that if the bride is not marrying from home but instead at a special location, perhaps staying in a hotel, the entire bridal party should be within 20 minutes of the venue for the service as well.

It is probably worth exploring the availability of local hotel rooms, even at this early stage, if you have guests coming from some distance, and making some reservations in case later the hotels are found to be full.

Passports

Brides and civil partners

Most brides choose to take their husband's surname on marriage and will therefore wish to change their name on their passport. In fact, it is perfectly legal to continue to use your passport in your maiden name until your current passport expires. Exactly the same applies if you are entering a civil partnership and wish to take your partner's name. If you are marrying abroad, it is useful to continue with your original passport so that it matches your travel tickets. You can also show your marriage certificate if required. You can change your passport as soon as you return home.

If your wedding is UK-based but you are honeymooning abroad, you can apply for a ten-year passport, post-dated in your new name, up to three months before your wedding. You will need to submit your current passport along with your application form, and this passport will then be cancelled, which means that you can no longer use it for travel between your application and your wedding. You can only use your new passport when the wedding has taken place. Be aware that the consulates of some countries will not issue visas on post-dated passports. You are advised to check with the consulate of the country you are travelling to. Security is much tighter these days and you don't want any delays or complications as you set off.

To apply early, you will be required to give your original birth certificate – not a photocopy – and a PD2 form, which must be filled in by your registrar, minister or priest. These forms are available from main post offices and from the Passport Information Line (0870 521 0410) which is also immensely helpful for any of your queries. There's a useful website too: www.passport.gov.uk.

To apply after your marriage, you will be required to present both your birth certificate and marriage certificate, as original documents. The forms for your change of name can be filled in online via the Home Office's Identity and Passport Service website.

Family and friends

If the wedding is going to be abroad, this is the time to check *everyone's* passports. There are some countries that insist that passports cannot be used within six months of their expiry date. You really don't want to be in a position where, at the last minute, it is discovered that someone in the immediate circle has only five months and 20 days left on their current passport.

Allow at least three weeks for a postal application for a new passport or a renewal, more to be on the safe side. There are quicker options: there is a two-week service available via certain post offices and a fast-track service by appointment only at the counters in passport offices (London, Liverpool, Peterborough and Glasgow). There's also a premium service for same-day collection, which, like the fast-track service, requires you to make an appointment and attend in person. However, this service is only for renewals and amendments, not entirely new applications. Be sure to take your original birth certificate with you when attending an appointment.

Again, the Home Office's Identity and Passport Service website: www.passport.gov.uk is extremely useful and offers online applications.

Passport photos

Your passport application can be delayed if your photographs are not acceptable.

You will require two identical photographs, 45 mm by 35 mm, which have been taken within the previous month of the application. Backgrounds must be pale – off-white, cream or pale grey – and completely plain. Even small children must appear on their own, without dummies or toys. You are required to show face and neck area, full front and formal (no wide smiles). Head coverings are only allowed for religious reasons but, obviously, the face must be uncovered. Other kinds of hats, shadows from glasses, dark tinted glasses and hair that falls across the eyes will not be accepted.

Visas and other overseas documents

This will be mentioned again in Chapter 9, but be sure to check what the requirements are for:

- documentation for the bride and groom
- entry visas for the bride, groom and family and friends attending the wedding.

3 Setting the budget

By now you should already be getting a feel of the scale and the 'style' of wedding that you and your families want. It's at this stage that a realistic master plan and budget can be put together.

Who pays for what

In the past, the tradition in Christian weddings – and it seemed to have leaked across to civil ones too – used to be:

The bride's family pays for:

- the bride's dress, bridesmaids' and pageboys' wedding clothes
- the wedding invitations and order-of-service sheets
- the transport of the bridal party (other than the groom and best man) to the wedding venue and on to the reception
- the reception itself, including the catering and wedding cake
- the official photography and videography.

The bride pays for:

- her pre-wedding party (hen night or similar celebration)
- a wedding ring for the groom
- her going away outfit.

The bridegroom pays for:

- the engagement ring
- the pre-wedding party (stag night or similar celebration)
- the bride's wedding ring
- wedding gifts for bridesmaids and pageboys
- the honeymoon.

The bridegroom's family pays for:

- the bridegroom's outfit
- ushers' outfits
- registrar or church fees (minister, verger, organist, choir, musicians, bell-ringers)
- the bride's and bridesmaids' flowers
- buttonholes/corsages for the rest of the bridal party
- wedding gifts for the best man and ushers
- transport for the bridegroom and best man to the ceremony.

It is up to the couple, and families concerned, to decide if they wish to follow this traditional pattern. In reality, nowadays these expenses are often split more evenly between the families. In many instances, the couple themselves, particularly if they are both working, undertake some or even most of the costs.

Costs to consider

Whether you are following the traditional pattern of splitting the budget or not, it's now time to consider what the costs under the various headings above may be. One way to do this is to set a figure and start drafting a budget, allowing that to dictate the size of the wedding, and the elements you decide to put around them. Alternatively, the couple and their families may wish for a specific size of event – very intimate with close family only, or a splashy large affair – and will look for ways to make that happen whatever the budget.

Likely expenses

Let's consider the likely expenses. Some of these items will be optional.

- The stag or hen parties: these can range from a night out with the boys to exotic weekends away. Often the bride's and bridegroom's friends pay for themselves. However, if there are mother-and-bride trips to a health spa, for instance, it may be appropriate to add them to the main budget.
- Stationery:
    - save the day cards (*optional*)
    - invitations
    - reply cards (*optional*)
    - service sheets
    - name place cards for the reception
- Event insurance (*optional*)
- Registrar's fees
- Minister's fees
- Service additions:
    - verger (Christian weddings)
    - music (organist or small group)
    - choir
    - bells/bell-ringers
- Wedding rings
- Presents for bridesmaids, pageboys, best man and ushers
- Transport for:
    - bride and bridesmaids/pageboys to the service
    - bridegroom and best man to the service
    - bride and bridegroom to reception

- bridesmaids and best man to reception
- bride and bridegroom going away.
- You may also wish to provide a bus, coach, minibus or taxis for guests staying at hotels or for taking people from the service to the reception party so they don't have to take private transport.

- Photography

- Videography

- Flowers/decoration:
  - bride's bouquet
  - bridesmaids' posies and corsages
  - buttonholes for bridegroom, best man, ushers, and close relatives
  - in the service venue
  - at the reception

- Wedding clothes and hairdressing:
  - bride's dress, veil, hat or headdress, shoes
  - bridesmaids' and pageboys' outfits
  - bridegroom's outfit
  - best man's and ushers' outfits
  - close relatives' outfits
  - hairdressing for main bridal party

- The reception party:
  - hall, room or marquee hire
  - catering: food and drink
  - wedding cake
  - toastmaster (*optional*)
  - music (band, dance floor)

- You may also wish to include taxis or minibuses for guests to return to their homes/hotels

- The honeymoon.

VAT

As you are sketching out your budget, remember that many of the services will be VAT-rated and your costings must allow for that. At the same time, check and double-check exactly what goods and services you are buying to ensure that there are no hidden extra costs.

Deposits

Be aware that some goods and services will require a deposit payable in advance. This may include flowers and catering. You may wish to create a schedule of costs across the months prior to your wedding.

Event insurance

As weddings are costly affairs and open to all kinds of mishaps, wedding insurance has become increasingly popular. It is easily available from at least one major high street chain and via a number of insurance companies.

Wedding insurance can cover items such as:

- cancellation (although this often excludes any decision by the bride and groom not to marry)
- loss or damage to the wedding clothes of the bridal party
- loss or damage to rings, presents, cake and flowers
- photography or videography, should the photographer not turn up or there is damage to the film
- lost deposits or additional costs if suppliers go into liquidation
- loss of transport
- loss of documents.

Some policies will also cover, if required, damage to marquees, public liability in case of damage to a guest's property or injury to them, and legal expenses.

4 Religious ceremonies: Christian

As in all faiths, there are wide differences in approach within the Christian faith: from the highly traditional churches of Greek and Russian Orthodoxy and Roman Catholicism, with their very elaborate rituals, to the simplicity of non-conformism. The sections below under 'Anglican' contain many of the practical requirements that are common to almost all Christian weddings, and therefore you may find it worth reading the chapter in its entirety and pulling out those elements that are applicable to your ceremony.

Anglican

Preparation

Most ministers prefer couples to undertake some form of preparation. This is a preparation for marriage rather than for the wedding itself and some priests even refer to it as marriage exploration. In some churches, small groups of couples come together; in others, the preparation is with individual couples. The number and length of the sessions will be by agreement.

Subject areas will vary from couple to couple. Some people may have delicate personal issues that they wish to explore in a 'safe' environment, such as bereavement, alcoholism and other dependencies. Others may have concerns about step-parenting or ageing parents – or about ageing themselves.

The Reverend Andrew Body has written extensively for couples who are marrying. In his latest book, *Making the most of weddings*, he says of preparation: 'Courses come and go, and no one size fits all. However, if a course does not cover the Big C's – Commitment, Communication and Conflict, then it is not going to be valuable.' His book *Growing together* is a valuable guide for all couples, covering topics ranging from dreams and expectations to money and sex. In each instance he asks couples to tackle the questions: 'Where are we coming from?', 'Where are we now?' and 'Where are we going?'. Both his books are published by Church House Publishing (www.chpublishing.co.uk).

Meeting your minister

The Revd Guy Bridgewater, vicar and team rector of Horsham, is keen that couples realise that the minister is there to facilitate the wedding and to make it a very special, meaningful and happy occasion:

Some people find the first meeting quite scary because it may be their first contact with the Church in many years. We are not there to criticise if you are not a regular church-goer nor are we going to make moral judgements if, for example, you have been living together. It is our privilege to get to know you. However, it is useful to make the minister aware of any family dilemmas if they might affect the atmosphere of the day. We can sometimes help keep the balance.

At the church or chapel

The minister will advise you in advance about if and how the church or chapel may be decorated with flowers, garlands and ribbons. Cathedrals, some churches and chapels will have a guild of flower arrangers, although you can usually choose whether you ask them to create your flowers or whether you bring someone in from outside.

In some churches, the dimensions of floral arrangements may be laid down. It is also worth remembering that there might be several weddings on the same day which would therefore require a change – or sharing – of floral decorations. It is usually much appreciated if you leave the flowers in place for the congregations the following day to enjoy.

In churches where there are bells, the cost and availability of ringers may be an element to consider. Usually there are peals to welcome the bride and again at the end of the service.

The verger's duties play an important part in your day. It is the verger's role to prepare the church or chapel: putting out the kneelers, hymn books, collection plates, microphones, the register and pens.

Other considerations include the use of confetti: some prefer no confetti at all, others will prescribe the use of biodegradable confetti only. There should also be a debate about when and where photography and video recordings are permissible, and this will apply to both amateurs and professionals. A number of ministers feel strongly that there are certain points within the service when filming and flash photography would be intrusive. We discuss this further in Chapter 14.

It is also worth considering at a fairly early stage the car parking for guests and for the to-ing and fro-ing of the bridal party's cars, since many churches and chapels were built in the days of carriages and shanks's pony! Again, having dealt with this situation many times, the minister may be able to tell you how to overcome problems of very limited car parking space.

Check too on wheelchair access and the arrangements for toilets, particularly if there will be children attending. Some chapels and churches also offer crèche facilities. Others can open their church halls for teas and coffees before the service for guests who have travelled long distances or afterwards for those not attending the main reception.

Service sheets

Deciding the form of the service in advance gives you plenty of time to put together the service sheet. Often the minister will help you to give it the correct layout and there may be choices to be made, for instance, whether to include the wording of the vows. Some churches offer to print the service sheets for you at a small charge. If you are having them specially printed by outside printers, be aware that not only should you check the proofs but also your minister will wish to do so too. If you are marrying in a historic or particularly interesting church or chapel, you may wish to include some details about it in the service sheets.

The form of service

For Anglo-Catholics, there is the option of a nuptial mass. The majority of people do not take up this option and choose instead the more usual order-of-service which is laid down in *Common Worship* or whatever service book your church or chapel uses. However, there is usually flexibility for the couple to make the ceremony individual, with touches that have special meaning for them. This includes the choice of readings and readers, the hymns, and music before and after the service and during the signing of the register.

Most ministers will ask for at least one of the readings to be from the Bible. (See the panel on page 34 for the most frequently requested Bible readings). If you have a particular poem or reading that you feel you would like to use for the second reading, show it to your minister. He will advise whether it is suitable or not. Ensure that any relatives or friends you ask to undertake the readings are fully comfortable with doing so. Not everyone is an actor and enjoys standing up before a crowd of even the most well-disposed people. Remember that actors always rehearse – and rehearse again – so be sure to give any reading to the reader well in advance so they can practise.

It is always advisable to have popular hymns at a wedding. A more obscure choice may mean that few people join in and the singing sounds weak. A good old-fashioned favourite ensures that everyone raises the roof. Some hymns have a number of different tunes to which they are sung. Double-check that the hymn you have chosen is to the tune you would like. In most venues, there will be the opportunity to have an organist, but be aware that this will incur a modest fee. In some churches, there may also be the option of having a choir, and the minister will explain the costs and implications of this to you. Not all choir members will be readily available on a Saturday, simply because they will be required the following day for services. Check with the choir director. It will probably be acceptable to ask friends with good voices and some musical background to supplement the resident choir.

Decisions also have to be made about the music to which the bride processes, and to accompany the newly married couple after the ceremony. There will also be a 'gap' in the service when the couple goes to sign the register. Again there will be options: this may include recorded music if there is a PA system installed, or having a music group, or inviting gifted friends or family to sing or play.

Rehearsal

Most ministers expect a rehearsal in the church or chapel for the bride and bridegroom and those participating in the service such as the bride's escort, best man, bridesmaids and readers of the lessons. For the latter it is a chance to practise and perhaps to learn how to use a microphone (where provided). If possible, it is a good idea to include parents and ushers as well. It helps to ensure that everyone knows what to do and when and where to do it.

It may also be valuable to time the sequence of the ceremony for the benefit of your official photographer and videographer and the minister will wish to tell them where they can stand and when they can move around without disrupting the atmosphere or dignity of the service.

Before the service

The ushers – two relatives or friends for a small wedding, up to six for a larger one – will guide guests to their seats. Traditionally, the bride's family and friends are seated on the left hand side facing the altar, the groom's family and friends are on the right. Front rows are usually reserved for close family members on the bride's side, and for the groom and his best man on the right.

Brides and their party are greeted at the door by the minister. They may choose to be escorted down the aisle, often by a father, brother or close family friend, although the traditional 'giving away' is optional. Many brides are accompanied by bridesmaids, matrons of honour (that is, married women acting as bridesmaids) or pageboys. Sometimes one of the bridesmaids or a pageboy will carry a small cushion on which the wedding rings are placed. The chief bridesmaid will take the bride's bouquet when she joins her groom. With couples marrying for a second time or for the renewal of wedding vows, the couple may decide to come in together.

The service itself

At the core of the ceremony is the exchanging of rings and the vows made holding hands. The congregation will recognise this and the minister will ensure that they understand the solemnity of this part of the service.

The Revd Guy Bridgewater adds:

The thing to remember is that you cannot really get it wrong. It doesn't matter if you fluff the words. The congregation will love it because they love the couple

The vows

You can, if you wish, ask for the archaic but beautiful vows which end 'thereto I plight thee my troth'. To plight was once a solumn oath, and the troth refers to faithfulness. However, the most usual vows nowadays are:

I (name), take you (name)
to be my wife (or husband)
to have and to hold
from this day forward:
for better, for worse,
for richer, for poorer,
in sickness and in health,

to love and to cherish,
till death us do part,
according to God's holy law.
In the presence of God, I make this vow.

And on the exchange of rings:

(Name), I give you this ring
as a sign of our marriage.
With my body I honour you,
all that I am I give to you,
and all that I have I share with you
within the love of God,
Father, Son and Holy Spirit.

Celebratory tale: Luci and Marcus

Luci and Marcus lived together for eight years with no plans to marry. Then, on holiday in California, Marcus surprised Luci with a cliff-top proposal and an engagement ring. She accepted.

At first they considered marrying in Italy which held special memories for them, but because of the costs for family and friends, they opted for the traditional route. Although living in London, they chose the parish church close to Marcus's parents' home in Northamptonshire, an area in which they had both grown up. They already knew the vicar from Christmas visits and their first move was to make an appointment with him.

The meeting covered three aspects: the legal requirements of residency within the parish for 15 consecutive days before the wedding, usually in the period of the calling of the banns; the practical arrangements and form of service, and then the pastoral element relating to the couple's personal relationship.

The form of service was important to both Marcus and Luci.

As a musician, Luci felt strongly about the choice of music, and arranged for a trumpeter and oboist as well as the organist, all of whom had family connections.

The couple carefully selected their readings: from the Song of Songs as their Biblical reading, a Shakespeare sonnet and a famous Irish blessing, and they asked Luci's godmother, her uncle and Marcus's sister to read for them. 'I found the readings incredibly emotional on the day,' says Luci.

Marcus and Luci had decided on a small wedding of 100, plus children. There were contributions from both sides of the family but the couple paid many of the costs, and undertook some tasks themselves, including making the invitations and service sheets. As they pointed out, this both saved money and set their own stamp on the occasion.

Luci asked her cousin to be her bridesmaid – 'she was such a lot of help, a marvellous sounding board throughout' – and had two small nieces as flower girls and a nephew as a pageboy. A cousin volunteered to do the video, but a professional photographer was commissioned.

The rehearsal was held on the day prior to the wedding, not just with the couple but also Luci's mother, who was giving her away, and her bridesmaid, the best man and most of Marcus's family, since they lived so close.

Their reception was held in a marquee in the grounds of a nearby manor house, which enabled guests to walk from the church. Luci's surprise for Marcus was a horse-drawn carriage ride. 'It was fun and it also gave us a short time to ourselves before we were meeting and greeting everyone,' she says.

They enjoyed the reception line, and one of their ushers acted as toastmaster. They had chosen not to have a top table, but instead circular tables – each named after a favourite holiday destination – with the main bridal party in the centre. This dealt with seating issues, since both the bride and groom's parents had divorced and remarried or had new partners.

Luci had made the wedding favours herself along with a personalised goodies bag for each child guest, with sweets and bottles of bubbles for the smallest and toys for the older ones. She also placed disposable cameras on each table, which the children enjoyed.

'It really was the happiest day of our lives,' says Luci.

Luci and Marcus's advice:

Plan it out carefully beforehand; don't leave anything until the last few days. Choose your caterer, florist and photographer with care so that you can just leave them to get on with it. You can then spend time making the day special to you. What matters is that it doesn't become a manufactured event, just another nice party, but something unique to be shared with your partner, family and loved ones.

Church of Scotland

There are slight differences in doctrine within the Church of Scotland. Marriage is not seen as a sacrament and binding for ever. Therefore remarriage is permitted, where one or both partners is divorced with their previous spouse still living.

Marriage in Scotland comes under Scottish law, and anyone who satisfies the requirements may be married in Scotland. For information about the legal requirements for both church and civil weddings, visit www.gro-scotland.gov.uk

Church of Scotland ministers may conduct weddings in venues other than their churches. This is a point of discussion and negotiation. A minister may feel that a certain venue does not lend itself to the meaning of the ceremony. Local ministers must be consulted where the marriage is between people living outside of Scotland. On a practical level, the minister may not be able to agree, simply because some locations are in such very high demand.

Methodist and Baptist

In the 'free' or non-conformist churches, a minister acts as an authorised person on behalf of a registrar and couples need to register at the local registry office and obtain a certificate in advance. The marriage can only go ahead if that certificate is given to the minister. On most other points weddings are similar and reflect the very special spiritual element of a Christian marriage.

Roman Catholic

Practising Catholics may marry in church and so can those who have not attended church for some time. It is also possible for Catholics to marry non-Catholics, whether they belong to another Christian denomination, another faith or have no religious belief at all. The priest will arrange permission or 'dispensation' if you are marrying a non-Catholic. He will also ask the Catholic partner to make a declaration as part of the preparation: 'I declare that I am ready to uphold my Catholic faith and to avoid all dangers of falling away from it. Moreover I sincerely undertake that I will do all that I can, within the unity of our partnership, to have all the children of our marriage baptised and brought up in the Catholic Church.'

Catholic weddings require a registrar's certificate, which means planning your civil ceremony in advance (see page 47 on civil ceremonies) unless your venue has special arrangements for registration. You will also be able to discuss with the priest whether you wish for a Nuptial Mass or a full ceremony but without the Mass and Holy Communion, and as with all wedding ceremonies, your priest will help you to decide appropriate readings, hymns and music.

Marriage Care, a charity whose aim is to support marriage, offers a very useful little booklet, *Marriage & Catholics*. See the website on www.marriagecare.org.uk.

The Religious Society of Friends

The Religious Society of Friends (the Quakers) have always brought their worship down to its essence. Often weddings take place within the normal weekly meeting of Friends, although there is provision to solemnise weddings in both private homes and hospitals, if one of the partners is seriously ill or incapacitated.

When a meeting is gathered in worship, each of the couples will stand and make their declaration. For a man this would be:

Friends, I take this, my friend (name) to be my wife, promising, through divine assistance, to be unto her a loving and faithful husband, as long as we both on earth shall live.

A woman makes the same declaration to her new husband.

Bible readings

There is usually an option regarding which translation of the Bible you prefer. Some people will opt for the King James Bible, others for a more modern version. The following are all taken from the Revised Standard Version.

Song of Solomon 2, 10–13

My beloved speaks and says to me:
'Arise, my love, my fair one,
and come away:
for now the winter is passed,
the rain is over and gone.

The flowers appear on the earth;
the time of singing has come,
and the voice of the turtle-dove
is heard in our land.
The fig tree puts forth its figs,
and the vines are in blossom;
they give forth fragrance.
Arise, my love, my fair one,
and come away.

1 Corinthians, 13
This includes the beautiful description of love:

Love is patient; love is kind; love is not envious or boastful or arrogant or rude. It does not insist on its own way; it is not irritable or resentful; it does not rejoice in wrongdoing, but rejoices in the truth. It bears all things, believes all things, hopes all things, endures all things.

John 2, 1–11
This is the wedding in Cana at which Jesus turned the water into wine.

You will find many more examples of readings in a sister publication, *Perfect Readings for Weddings*.

5 Religious ceremonies: Jewish – Muslim – Hindu – Sikh

What is so delightful about all the wedding customs described here is the cultural overlap. At the heart of each kind of ceremony are the promises and commitment of the couple who are marrying, the sharing of the celebration with families and friends, the symbolism of the new journey and the new home that the couple will make. In every instance there is the wish to make the event a very special occasion, with treats and gestures of generosity and meaning.

The Jewish tradition

The usual venue for Jewish weddings is the synagogue, but weddings can be conducted in other venues, such as hotels, outdoor spaces, or places that have special meaning. Kirsty and Morris, for example (see page 60) were married at The Gatsby Suite at Pinewood Studios, where Morris frequently works.

During the ceremony all men present will be asked to cover their heads with the traditional Jewish cap, the *kippah*. In the Orthodox branches of the Jewish faith, it is preferred that women guests cover their shoulders and arms. Traditionally, all women's heads should be covered. Men will sit in the body of the synagogue, while women guests sit in the balcony.

It is the custom for Jewish brides to wear either white or ivory to symbolise purity. Nowadays, many will be attended by bridesmaids. It is customary for the bride and bridegroom not to see one another for at least a day before their wedding and to fast on their wedding day until after the ceremony.

Before the wedding ceremony, there are two rites: the signing of the *ketubah*, the formal marriage contract where the bridegroom accepts responsibilities for the maintenance of his bride according to Jewish law. The *ketubah* is read out to the bridegroom, who then signs it before two witnesses, who then also sign to validate it. The bridegroom is then escorted to see his bride. He will draw the veil from his bride's face so he can see that she is the woman he has chosen to marry. This is a private ceremony with only the closest family present.

The couple then proceed to the wedding canopy, the *chupah*, which symbolises the home that they will make together. It is open on its four sides to welcome guests from all four corners of the earth, showing that their new home will be equally welcoming.

Under the *chupah*, the bride circles the bridegroom seven times as a symbol of the protection and care she will offer him. As God created the world in seven days, so the bride is building the walls of the couple's new world together. The symbol of the bridegroom's care and protection comes with the wedding ring, made from precious but unadorned metal, that he will now place on the forefinger of the bride's right hand, saying in Hebrew: 'Behold you are betrothed unto me with this ring according to the laws of Moses and Israel.' At this point, the couple are fully married. Nuptial blessings follow, in the last of which the groom rejoices with his bride, surrounded by joy, gladness, delight and cheer, love and harmony, peace and friendship. The groom then stamps on a glass, wrapped in cloth, to recall the destruction of the temple in Jerusalem, a reminder that even in joyful times, the sorrows of the Jewish people are not forgotten. At the conclusion of the ceremony, the couple will spend a few moments in total privacy before the reception party.

Many Jewish weddings take place in the afternoon, and the reception that follows takes the form of a meal, probably with a dance afterwards. The customs are very similar to the Christian tradition, with a top table, speeches and a wedding cake, and wedding favours for guests.

The Muslim tradition

Traditionally, Muslim marriages were arranged between families. Nowadays the families still play a part, but it is usually considered essential that both partners meet, get to know one another and then decide if they are capable of making a happy union.

Practices and customs differ between the different branches of the Islamic faith and between those who come from an Indian background or an African or Arabic background. The Muslim faith allows for intermarriage with other 'People of the Book', that is, Christians and Jews, but would not permit marriage with anyone from other faiths such as Hindu or Shinto. The first requirement of couples of mixed faith therefore is to seek guidance from their local priest.

A civil service at a registry office is required, followed by the religious ceremony at the Islamic centre or mosque. Ideally, the couple would marry on a Thursday evening or a Friday, since these are the holy days of the week, or on a religious holiday. However it has become more practical for couples to marry at a weekend, simply so that more of their friends and family are available to attend the celebrations.

The bride often holds a henna party before her wedding, with her female relatives and friends. Often there will be a religious talk and advice about marriage given during the evening, as well as the painting of the bride's hands with henna.

Muslim brides favour white for their wedding outfit – a sari or, more usually, the three-piece *shalwar*, *kameez* and *dupatta* – but may also wear red or other colours. They will be attended by at least one adult bridesmaid and by the small girls of the family, all resplendent in their wedding attire. While the wedding costs are usually shared between the families, it is customary for the bridegroom to pay for his bride's wedding clothes, including her jewellery. One Muslim bride, Zahra, opted for red for her sari, and her bridegroom, Abbas, who wore a suit, reflected her choice in the red of his tie. 'And he spent *ages* trying to find that tie,' his mother-in-law said with amusement.

At the Islamic centre or mosque, the bride, her attendants and all the women guests will sit in one chamber while the bridegroom, his best man and all the male guests sit in another. The women's chamber will usually have video and audio links, so they can witness the proceedings.

The ceremony begins with a marriage sermon which invites the bride and bridegroom to a life of piety, mutual love, kindness and social responsibility. At the core of the wedding celebration is the recitation of the marriage contract, the *Nikah*. The *Nikah* is a tri-lateral contract between the bride, bridegroom and God. It is made in Arabic and, if the bride and bridegroom are not fluent, they may each appoint a representative who is. The two representatives will then make the declaration before the assembled guests.

The second part of the celebration is the party. This can be very simple, kept to just close family or friends, or it can be something very much larger. At Zahra and Abbas's wedding party, there were at least 1,500 guests. The party has many and varied traditions, according to where the family comes from, but a frequent one is the cutting of the cake, where the bride and bridegroom, now officially married, come together. They may also exchange rings at this point, although in some instances the rings have already been given at the civil ceremony.

After a few hours, the couple will retire and seek privacy.

A favourite Muslim prayer:

O Allah! Bond their hearts as You did between that of Adam and Eve.

O Allah! Bond their hearts as You did between that of Abraham and Sara.

O Allah! Bond their hearts as You did between that of Your beloved Muhammad and the illustrious Khadija.

O Allah! Bond their hearts as You did between that of Ali and Fatima Zahra.

O Allah! Grant them good sustenance and noble children, Indeed You have power over everything.

The Hindu tradition

Dr Raj Pandit Sharma, head of the Hindu Priests Association in the UK, explains that the Hindu faith sanctions the marriage of all individuals, regardless of race, religious belief (or lack of it) and nationality. Unlike other faiths, the couple does not have to convert to Hinduism or even be adherents, to have this kind of marriage. Therefore a mixed faith marriage is perfectly permissible.

Traditionally Hindu couples had their astrological charts matched by the family priest to confirm their compatibility. This ancient science has been used for centuries and its success can be judged by relatively low divorce rates. These days, the couple will have met and decided to marry before this stage but, frequently, natal charts are still matched and preventative remedies introduced before the ceremony, ensuring a harmonious future for the couple.

There is a pre-betrothal stage when friends and family meet and formally announce the forthcoming marriage. The couple's natal charts are examined again to select auspicious dates for the wedding. The formal engagement takes place only a few days before the wedding, when the groom's family invite the bride's family to their home, along with close family and friends, for a religious ceremony, praying to the Almighty in the form of Lord Ganesh, the remover of obstacles, to grant success to the couple. Gifts are exchanged – from the bride's family to the groom, and the groom's family to the bride. She receives jewellery, clothes, sweets, fruits and cosmetics and a highly embroidered large veil, the '*dupatta/chunni*'. This represents the groom's family honour and officially acknowledges that she is to become his wife.

In the past, weddings were held in the bride's home, but nowadays this is not practical given the numbers of guests who usually attend. All sorts of venues are permissible: a marquee, palace, castle, country club, botanical garden, large hotel and so on. The temple is not always ideal, since many temples forbid the consumption of alcohol and the serving of non-vegetarian food, and some priests do not speak English. Many couples prefer a priest capable of translating the ceremony for the benefit of their non-Indian speaking guests.

Arrangements range from the simple to the spectacular and many families opt for the assistance of a wedding planner. Wedding clothes and jewellery in a Hindu wedding are paramount and both men and women dress extravagantly in magnificent silks and other fabrics in dazzling colours. The bride's outfit is usually crimson, accessorised with gold or diamond jewellery. White is not considered auspicious, as it is the colour of mourning in the Hindu faith. The groom's attire is equally impressive and varies according to regional tradition. A long silk shirt (*kurta*) and pyjama or *dhoti* (male equivalent of a sari) is common. A long round-collared coat resembling a morning coat known as a *sherwani* is quite popular.

It is quite common for the groom to wear a headdress, such as a turban, and in North Indian traditional Hindu families the turban is bound by a pure silver 'crown' or *mukut*. The face of the groom would be obscured by the *sehra*, which consists of an elaborate headband, from which long tassels extend. The groom would also wear a long sash of a fine material that is draped over the neck, both ends extending to just above the knees.

The core of the religious ceremony is usually condensed to just over one hour, and again there are regional and cultural variations. However, the main points are as follows.

The parents, relatives and friends of the bride welcome the groom and his entourage and the groom proceeds to the marriage podium, the *mandap*.

The bride's parents honour the groom by presenting him with items reserved for most revered guests, including *madhuparka*, a beverage composed of yoghurt, honey and ghee, which gives vitality and good health.

The bride enters, accompanied by her bridesmaids. She exchanges garlands with the groom, expressing the couple's free and mutual desire to be married.

The scarves of the bride and groom are then tied, symbolising their spiritual union. *Kanyadaan* is perhaps the most significant part of the ceremony. The bride's father places the hand of his daughter in that of the groom and declares that at this auspicious hour, with his own free will and that of the bride, he hereby gives permission for his daughter to marry the groom. The bride and the groom then clasp hands and make solemn vows to love and cherish one another.

The sacred fire is kindled and, with the recitation of Vedic hymns or mantras, the priest assists the bride and groom to celebrate the marriage sacrifice by making offerings into the fire.

Among the other rites, the bride and groom will circumambulate the sacred fire seven (or four) times in a clockwise motion, at the same time affirming their vows. The couple make the following seven mutual agreements whilst taking seven steps together:

Let us promote wellbeing and good health
Let us mutually develop physical and mental strength
Let us create wealth through ethical and honourable means
Let us be blessed with progeny
Let us be respectful to all creeds and creatures
Let us be content through all walks of life
Let us be true friends and remain faithful to one another

The groom then places vermilion powder in the bride's hair parting, signifying her status as a married woman, and gives her the marriage necklace as the priest recites verses from the Vedas. The assembly joins the priest, blessing the couple by showering them with flower petals and sacred rice.

During the ceremony, when the groom accepts the bride's hand in marriage, the following Sanskrit verse is recited on his behalf, describing the immortal concept of love transcending physical parameters.

Who has given this heart and to whom?
Love has given unto love.
Love is the giver and love is the receiver.
Love has entered the ocean of love.

I receive you through love.
O' love, this heart is yours.

(Kathaka-Samhita, 9.9.12)

The Sikh tradition

Traditionally, Sikh marriages are still arranged by the families, but both partners must be agreeable. By and large, what has evolved is more of a match-
making service with a national network of aunts and grannies letting people
know who is available, and exchanging photographs of potential brides and
bridegrooms. According to PR consultant Daljit Bhurji, young Asians are
now taking the matter of finding partners into their own hands and there is a
huge growth of matrimonial internet sites. As he points out, weddings themselves are prime hunting grounds for contact with a potential partner.

According to the Sikh Code, anyone who is not of the Sikh faith
cannot be married by the formal Sikh marriage ceremony, the *Anand
Karaj*. Sikh marriages are monogamous and divorce is not allowed.

The weddings usually take place around midday, either in the home
of the bridegroom or at the Sikh temple. An engagement ceremony is
not considered necessary but, where desired, usually takes place a week
before the wedding, again either at the bridegroom's home or the
temple. The families greet each other, exchanging garlands, and there is
a simple ceremony of hymns and prayers. A traditional meal follows.
Often the bride's family will have gifts for the groom, while they are pre-
sented with an Indian outfit and sweets for their daughter.

If you wish to marry in your local temple, it will be registered for the
solemnisation of marriages, but it is wise to book the date as early as
possible. Any day is considered auspicious for a wedding, which usually
start in the morning.

There are different customs among Sikh families for who helps the
bride prepare for her wedding. Sometimes the bride's closest female relatives and friends will stay with her in the days leading to the wedding,
and they will form a 'henna party', attending to her hair and painting her

hands, arms and legs with henna designs. While the bridegroom is often dressed in white, the bride will wear colourful robes, often in red with gold embroidery, and a full veil until after the ceremony.

In the morning, both sides of the family meet at the temple where a hall will be set up with tables and chairs, tea and refreshments. There then follows a cermony which (weather permitting) usually takes place outside, when the senior male family members take it in turns to meet their equivalents. This culminates with the two fathers or grandfathers, who traditionally exchange gold rings. They will then embrace and try to lift one another off the ground, often to the amusement of the crowd! The whole ceremony underlines how Sikh weddings are as much about the marriage of the two families as of the bride and groom.

Men and women will then sit on different sides, but within the same chamber. The marriage ceremony takes place with the bride sitting to the left of the bridegroom in front of the officiate, who will remind the couple of the duties and mutual obligations of married life according to the teachings of the Sixth Holy Scripture, *Sri Guru Granth Sahib*. The couple vow fidelity to each other before the assembly and bow to the Guru.

The core of the ceremony is very simple: the bride's father will place one end of the bridegroom's sash, or patka, over the couple's shoulders and into the bride's hands, symbolising her new life with her husband. The officiate then reads the four *lavan* (stanzas) from *Guru Granth Sahib*. Between each stanza, the couple will circumambulate slowly around the *Guru Granth Sahib*, the bridegroom leading the bride, accompanied by religious singers, the *ragis*. During the circling, the bride's brothers and male cousins stand spaced around the route, passing the bride between them, signifying that the bride is being given willingly to the groom.

At the completion of the ceremony, a holy poem is read, and the holy sweet pudding, *karah prashad*, is distributed to all the guests. The reception with food and dancing that follows can be a small affair or, as Daljit describes it, a cast of thousands.

In the evening, there is a final tradition where the bride returns to her family home to leave as the last time as a member of her family, an emotional occasion with many tears from the bride's family.

Celebratory tale: Bella and Andy

Bella and Andy had known each other for many years through college friends before finally coming together. Bella, who is not aligned to one particular religion now, came from a Hindu family, attended a Catholic school and was brought up to be totally integrated into British society. Andy is atheist, although his mother is a committed Methodist.

Bella says: 'On our own, we would probably have chosen a humanistic or alternative wedding but we wanted to please and involve our families. It meant a lot to my mother that I had an Indian wedding, but she would never have "made" us do so.'

In fact, they had two weddings: one Indian, the other a civil ceremony. Bella's mother, armed with their birth dates and times, consulted family and a guru in India to establish auspicious and convenient days for the wedding. One fell on a Friday, which the couple wanted, enabling them to hold the civil wedding on the following day.

'Hindu weddings can be enormous, with hundreds of guests in huge temples off the M25. We chose to have ours in a smaller temple, yards from our house, so we could limit it to about 200. We also negotiated down the length of the wedding, which can last several days, to about three hours! It was an ancient Vedic ceremony with much more focus on the natural forces – sun, moon, fire – than on deities,' Bella explains.

Bella's mother organised the occasion, including the catering. The temple priest conducted the ceremony, but she also arranged for a guru to come over from India. Bella's father prepared a written translation and explanation of the service so Andy's family and friends who were of other faiths could follow the proceedings. Bella wore the beautiful traditional bridal dress of red heavily embroidered silk, and, despite her feminist leanings, covered her hair. Andy made several visits to Southall, where he found a *kurta* and *shalwar* (which look like white silk long pyjamas), which he wore with a heavily embroidered maroon sleeveless overcoat and what he calls genie-in-the-lamp slippers. They were both touched that so many of their UK friends made an effort to wear coloured silks and Indian jewellery, and enjoyed dressing up and really got into the spirit of the whole thing.

Bella explains that the Hindu ceremony is very much about welcoming – and nurturing – each other and entering into a new phase of life with support from those around the couple. 'The ceremony, conducted in Sanskrit, is colourful, joyful and rich in the most beautiful and meaningful rituals. It involves lots of participation from friends and family, not just the couple.' She and Andy exchanged garlands, made from flowers flown over especially from India. They were married seated around a fire beneath a canopy (the *mandap*) where, central to all the rites and rituals, they made their vows to take care of each other, carry out their social and family obligations, raise virtuous children, always be truthful and loving, and live happily together until parted by death.

'It was an amazing spectacle. Bella looked beautiful, despite covering her hair, and I enjoyed dressing up myself,' says Andy. 'The following day Bella wore a white wedding dress for the civil ceremony and the reception that followed, and my family, some of whom hadn't met her prior to the weddings, had a chance to see her in Western dress.'

They both felt that they had reflected the best of both traditions. Bella and Andy's advice:

Know what you are doing and why you are doing it. If the wedding is just for yourself, design it exactly as you want it. But if you are also doing it for your families, you need to give up some of that control. Neither of us are strongly religious but we thoroughly enjoyed it all too. You can have a lot of fun going into an unfamiliar situation. There's no point in being too protective and angst-ridden. Be relaxed.

6 Non-religious ceremonies

There are all kinds of reasons why couples choose a non-religious wedding. Perhaps they come from different cultures or different faiths, or hold strong atheist beliefs. Maybe one or more of them has been divorced and the former spouse is still living. Or perhaps they are a same-sex couple who wish to form a civil partnership.

There are several options for designing a non-religious wedding. However, all of them start at the registry office. This is the ceremony that is accepted under British law, and sometimes is all that the couple require. However, some couples will decide to seek a service of blessing from their chosen church or chapel, while others will opt for a humanist service into which they can create a celebration that has meaning for both of them.

The registry office

The more formal part of applying to the registry office for a ceremony either in the registry offices themselves or in one of the listed approved venues is set out in Chapter 3.

It is important to remember that if you choose to marry in a registry office, the vows and any music and readings must have no religious connotation. This is strictly a civil event. However, this sounds all very formal, but in fact registrars are well aware of how important it is to personalise each and every wedding and they are always pleased to hear ideas of how to make the occasion unique to each couple.

If you wish, you can follow the form of a traditional wedding, with a procession of the bride, her escort, bridesmaids and pageboys. The groom can be attended by a best man. Alternatively you may choose to do none of these things, but arrive hand-in-hand with your partner.

In traditional church weddings, the bride's family and friends normally sit on the left facing the altar, with the groom's family and friends on the right. There is no real reason why you should follow this procedure at a civil ceremony, unless you wish to. Other than the closest relatives and anyone taking part in the service who obviously should be on the front row, you can allow your guests to find their own places or be directed by your ushers.

You can choose background music (usually a CD, but a small group of musicians has been known) for your entrance and for after the ceremony. Most registry offices and approved venues have music systems, and many will already have a selection of appropriate music too. If you choose the music yourself, it must be approved by your registrar in advance of the wedding. Similarly, you can ask for someone – a close relative or special friend – to give a reading but again, your registrar must approve the reading in advance. He or she will also help you decide how best to incorporate the reading and music into the ceremony.

The civil ceremony is laid down in the Marriage Acts and requires you to make one of two statements, either a declaratory statement or a contracting statement. Your registrar will discuss this with you. You will require two people – relatives or friends – to act as your witnesses.

After the ceremony, the bride and groom will be taken aside to sign the register in time-honoured fashion.

Photographs and videography are normally permitted both during the ceremony and the signing of the register. Check with your registrar about any restrictions relating to confetti. Some registry offices will only allow biodegradable confetti to be used.

Suzanne Brown, a registrar with the Cornwall Registration Service, says:

Some of the best weddings have been with just the couple and their two witnesses. I have felt a real sense of commitment from them and it's been all the more emotional.

Humanist weddings

A very interesting and increasingly common option is to consider a humanist wedding. Humanism is the belief that we can live good lives without religious or superstitious beliefs. By and large, it looks at how we behave in this life, rather than looking to the next.

Humanist ministers – also known as officiants, or celebrants – believe that they can offer a thoughtful and highly personal alternative, one that couples might not find in a registry office, where the timings are frequently tight and there are strict guidelines about how the ceremony is conducted and what can be said and done.

Humanist weddings can be held in virtually any venue, including outdoors – in a garden, on a mountainside, in a vineyard or on a beach – although attention should be paid to ensuring that the acoustics are appropriate and that there is a wet weather plan. Rupert Morris, a London-based humanist minister, recalls one wedding held in December on Richmond Hill, with several of the guests wearing Wellington boots. Fortunately he has a strong voice and the weather held, but it was a risk. He has also conducted ceremonies in other parts of Europe, including at the beautiful Villa Cimbrone in Ravello, on the Italian coast.

Usually several meetings precede the event. There will be a preliminary meeting to ensure that the couple are happy and comfortable with their particular minister. A further meeting will follow when the minister will fully explore the couple's beliefs and priorities, and their hopes for their relationship. From this discussion, they can then decide how the ceremony might come together, and look at those who might contribute towards it. For example, some couples may want to involve one or more of their parents or guardians, perhaps to give a blessing to the marriage or express a personal view of the bride and groom. They may have children and wish for them to participate in the ceremony. The minister will help the couple reflect their beliefs in the ceremony, find the kind of readings and music that they would find meaningful, and choose the form and wording of the vows they wish to exchange. A rehearsal is held whenever possible.

You will be able to find a humanist minister in your area by contacting the British Humanist Association (www.humanism.org.uk).

Here is an example of the vows exchanged by a couple, both in their 80s, one Christian, the other Jewish, at their humanist ceremony:

> *(name), I love and respect you;*
> *I would like you to share my life as I hope to share yours;*
> *I promise to treat you always as my equal*
> *And let you develop in your own way;*
> *I will try to be kind and understanding*
> *So that we may find fulfilment in our life together.*
> *I offer you this ring as a token of my love and regard.*

Civil partnerships

Same-sex couples have been able to gain legal recognition of their partnerships since December 2005. British gay and lesbian couples have campaigned for many years to gain legal recognition of their relationship and this culminated in the Civil Partnership Act 2004. The implications of the act are that same-sex couples who formally register now have the same rights as married couples in areas relating to inheritance, survivor pensions, life assurance, equal treatment for tax purposes, social security benefits and tax credits. They are also exempt from testifying against one another in court (like married couples) and have next of kin rights. A very useful website explaining the full benefits is www.stonewall.org.uk.

The situation is varied worldwide. In Canada, gay unions are referred to as marriages and have been legal for some years. In New Zealand, Civil Union ceremonies have given same-sex couples the same status as marriage since 2005 and South Africa legalized gay marriage in 2006, the first African country to do so. At the time of writing, Australia has a Civil Unions Bill in the Australian Capital Territory but it is not yet enacted. In other areas, some celebrants will officiate at a Commitment Ceremony.

Same-sex couples can decide whether to retain their names or take the name of one partner. This has implications, amongst other things, for passports (see page 15 about how to apply for a new passport if you are planning to change your name).

The procedure for registering a partnership is exactly the same as it is for straight couples. You will need to give formal notice in person at your local registry office, even if you choose to have the ceremony else-where. The ceremony can take place either within the registry office itself or one of its licensed venues. The only difference in procedure is the placing of the notice of intent to marry. In the case of straight cou-ples, details including names, addresses and occupations are published. This may raise some issues for same-sex couples, and so the registrar will only publish names and occupations but not addresses.

Most registry offices publish a little brochure about civil partnership ceremonies. There is a suggested form of words, but registrars stress that – as with any wedding – they welcome suggestions and ideas from the participants, which will make the occasion special and memorable. The only current prohibition is that there can be no religious references in the readings or music. If you wish to use music or a poem which has any words relating to religious subjects – to angels, to God and so on – you must show them to your registrar well in advance.

It is therefore up to the couple to add the dimensions that will make the event truly meaningful. The only legal requirement is for two wit-nesses to be present, but both registry offices and their licensed venues will accommodate much larger gatherings.

Same-sex couples can also consider having a humanist ceremony after the formal legal procedure at the registry office. There is still no legislation covering religious blessings and, at the time of writing, the picture remains patchy and unclear. The religious blessings of same-sex partnerships are still being considered by most churches and faiths. Some churches – for example, the Roman Catholic church and the Muslim tradition – are firmly opposed to any form of recognition. However, many other churches, often following fierce highly polarised debate, have a party line that forbids ministers or priests from giving such blessings, but it is known that individual priests are willing to do so. The advice here can only be for couples to discuss the matter with their churches. There is an alternative. The Metropolitan Community Churches are a worldwide network of churches, with their own ministers, which serve the gay community. See www.mccchurch.org.

Almost a quarter of couples elect to have their ceremony abroad and there are many countries where this presents no problem. There are others – Iran, Dubai and Jamaica, for instance – where homosexuality is illegal. It is wise to check before making any firm plans.

What is already clear is that same-sex couples are leading the way to more imaginative forms of commitment ceremony. They do not have to subscribe to the old traditions – some of which have become tired and lack significance – and are free to create entirely personal declarations and ceremonies of genuine meaning to everyone present.

There are now specialist gay wedding planners. One such is Pink Weddings. Director Gino Meriano explains: 'When the act first came into being, it was mainly older, long-established couples who were registering, quickly and quietly, simply in order to obtain the legal rights. Now, we are finding younger couples are coming forward and they want their union to be celebrated more publicly. Some are more outrageous than others, but by and large no one wants to turn such a special event into a freak show. After all, many same-sex couples have children. Most have families, and we are aware that some families – or some members of some families – find the occasion difficult.

'We often take the traditional but adapt it. We don't use the terms 'bride' and 'groom' and we tend not to go in for a single aisle at the service, but may put in two if, for example, two fathers wish to give away their daughters. Most couples prefer not to have a rectangular 'top table' at the reception but instead have round tables.'

His partner, Mike, adds: 'We were one of the first couples in England to have a ceremony, on the day the act came into force. We didn't fully appreciate the importance of it – it really was a Nelson Mandela moment – but society as a whole will take a bit longer to appreciate it.'

Celebratory tale: Andie and Ricky

Andie and Ricky had their civil partnership wedding in the first year of the act coming into force. They were mildly apprehensive about their first interviews with the local registrar but found the experience wholly positive and relaxed. They found the registrar was open to making the ceremony different, and while giving them ideas for readings and music, pointed out that they could choose their own as long as there was no religious connotation. Andie had wanted an Indian chant but it was explained that the lyrics might be religious and would have to be checked. This was becoming too complicated so he elected for another favourite song instead. They were given a choice of three vows, ranging from a straight 'I do' to something quite elaborate. The giving of their vows was the heart and serious side of the ceremony, while the rest was friendly, fun and informal.

Ricky explains that originally they had wanted a small, quick legal ceremony but found that friends were expecting a much bigger celebration that would have more meaning. As a result they chose a ceremony with close friends and family, followed by lunch, and a huge party in the evening to which everyone they knew was invited.

Andie and Ricky's advice:

Just because you are a same-sex couple, you do not have to wear the same outfits, otherwise you risk ending up looking like either funeral directors or ABBA. Keep the service simple and be extravagant with your party. Don't invite anyone to the ceremony who has qualms about gay weddings. Explain that the ceremony will be for close family and friends only; it will let them off the hook – but invite them to the 'do'.

Non-religious readings

Rupert Morris, minister of the British Humanist Association, has suggested the following as examples of non-religious readings:

Shakespeare's 116th sonnet

Let me not to the marriage of true minds
Admit impediments. Love is not love
Which alters when it alteration finds,
Or bends with the remover to remove:

O, no! It is an ever-fixed mark,
That looks on tempests and is never shaken;
It is the star to every wand'ring bark,
Whose worth's unknown, although his height be taken.

Love's not time's fool, though rosy lips and cheeks
Within his bending sickle's compass come;
Love alters not with his brief hours and weeks,
But bears it out even to the edge of doom,
If this be error and upon me prov'd,
I never writ, nor no man ever lov'd.

'On marriage' by Kahlil Gibran

Then Almitra spoke again and said, And what of Marriage, master?

And he answered saying:
You were born together, and together you shall be for evermore.
You shall be together when the white wings of death scatter your days.
Ay, you shall be together even in the silent memory of God.
But let there be spaces in your togetherness,
And let the winds of the heavens dance between you.

Love one another, but make not a bond of love:
Let it rather be a moving sea between the shores of your souls.
Fill each other's cup but drink not from one cup.
Give one another of your bread but eat not from the same loaf.
Sing and dance together and be joyous, but let each one of you be
   alone.
Even as the strings of a lute are alone though they quiver with the
   same music.

From an essay by Laurie Lee

Love must be built on truth, not dream, the knowledge of what we are, rather than what we think it is the fashion to be. For no pair of lovers, no pair of leaves, was ever built to an identical programme. So beware of the norm, for no one is normal.

The sum of love is that it should be a meeting-place, an interlocking of nerves and senses, a series of constant surprises and renewals of each other's moods, a sharing of the gods of bliss and silence – best of all, a steady building, from the inside out, from the cosy centre of love's indulgencies, to extend its regions to admit a larger world.

Love must be deep to adapt to the shifting sands of the world; sufficiently constant, in the centre of orgy and bedlam, to create its own area of sacred quiet.

For love still has intimations of immortality to offer us, if we are willing to pay it tribute. If we can learn to forget the old clichés of jealousy and pride and not be afraid to stand guard, protect, acquiesce, forgive, and even serve. Love is not merely the indulgence of one's personal taste-buds; it is also the delight in indulging another's. Also in remembering the lost beauties, perhaps briefly glimpsed in adolescence, of such simplicities as tenderness and care, in feeling able to charm without suffering loss of status, in taking some pleasure in the act of adoring, and in being content now and then to lie by one's sleeping love and to shield her eyes from the sun.

The closing words of a native American wedding ceremony

Now you will feel no rain
For each of you will be shelter for the other;
Now you will feel no cold
For each will be warmth to the other;
Now you will not be lonely
For although you are two persons, there is only one life before you.
Go now to your home to enter into your life together;
And may your days be good and long upon the earth.

An extract taken from the chapter 'Love' in *Life Lessons* by Elizabeth Kubler-Ross and David Kessler

Love, that thing we have great difficulty even describing, is the only truly real and lasting experience of life. It is the opposite of fear, the essence of relationships, the core of creativity, the grace of power, an intricate part of who we are. It is the source of happiness, the energy that connects us and that lives within us.

Love has nothing to do with knowledge, education, or power; it is beyond behaviour. It is also the only gift in life that is not lost. Ultimately, it is the only thing we can really give. In a world of illusions, a world of dreams and emptiness, love is the source of truth.

You will find many more examples of readings in a sister publication, *Perfect Readings for Weddings*.

7 Multicultural and mixed faith weddings

It's happening all the time. In our wonderfully mixed society, people from different cultural backgrounds and different faiths are meeting, falling in love, and deciding to make a future together. Sometimes the pairing is accepted easily, and family and friends help the new couple make any necessary adaptations to their particular traditions in order to celebrate the marriage. Sometimes the reaction is not quite so positive and requires some heart-searching, tolerance and compromise on behalf of one side or both sides of the families. Occasionally, such marriages cause rifts that cannot be bridged and that is very hard and very sad.

In terms of planning a wedding of two cultures but perhaps a common faith, or of two different faiths, the recipe for success seems to be in open discussion – with a large measure of sensitivity – about the expectations of both the bride and the groom, and then of their respective families. Communication and good humour is everything here. One good way forward is to acknowledge both cultures or both faiths in some meaningful way, rather than having one taking precedence. This makes it easier for the couple to maintain happy links with their respective in-laws in the future. If one side feels slighted, it can have a decidedly detrimental effect which may lead to future problems.

It becomes slightly more complicated if either the bride or groom comes from another country, which may mean that possibly only close relatives and friends are able to travel. Some couples solve this by having two ceremonies, one in this country, the second in the other. Others opt for a ceremony here but hold a reception or party abroad.

If the wedding is to be in the UK, there are a number of options:

- a straightforward civil ceremony in a registry office or one of its approved venues
- a civil ceremony, followed by a humanist wedding service
- a civil service followed by services of religious blessings.

Even where there is perfect accord about the kind of ceremony and the reception party, its location and format, success rests in the detail. What is acceptable in one culture may be considered offensive in another.

Different generations may have differing attitudes and, in order to maximise harmony, this must be taken into account. Younger generations may find other people's customs or forms of behaviour entirely accept-able while the older generation may be appalled at them. At the same time, the bride and groom's generation may find various traditions out-dated or even silly and may be unwilling to subscribe to them. Again, very open – and good humoured – discussion may be the best path. For exam-ple, if a grandmother is likely to be offended if some custom is not hon-oured, perhaps the bride and groom should visit her in advance to explain why it is inappropriate and to ask for her understanding. If a groom is required to wear a certain headdress or undertake a ritual which his friends may find hilarious, it is up to him to squash this kind of thought-lessness, again in advance. Leaving it all to chance may cause untold harm. Tackle the problems up front so you can relax and enjoy the day.

Cautionary tale: Florian and Gina

Respect the customs – and also the *wishes* – of both sides. Florian was Austrian, Gina was Italian, and both were Catholic. They were married in Vienna and their relatives and friends from all over Europe came to celebrate the event. At the reception party, Florian's family decided to play the games traditional in their society, including one where the bride was 'kidnapped' and the groom had to search for her – via all the local bars. This would take at least an hour or more. However, Gina refused to be 'kidnapped'. Not unnaturally, she wanted to spend as much time as possible introducing her new husband to the guests who had travelled so far. So Gina's family decided to 'kidnap' the groom instead. Gina was furious. Both bride and groom were by this stage upset by each other's behaviour – and their family's behaviour – and felt that the reception was spoiled.

Florian and Gina's advice:

Confirm beforehand which customs will – and what will not – be acceptable and, as important, ensure that the followers of both parties subscribe to it.

Hospitality

The catering for the reception party can hold challenges. Some traditions are largely vegetarian and some forbid alcohol. After the Quaker wedding I attended, a meal was offered, not because a reception party was their tradition but because so many guests had travelled long distances. It was only hospitable to feed us. Fine cider was offered for those who would enjoy it, although the Quakers, by and large, do not drink alcohol. Their courtesy was much appreciated.

Within some traditions, there may be some very special dishes attached to weddings. To incorporate at least some of these even if it is not your tradition would be both hospitable and gracious.

This, then, is perhaps the key. Make the wedding an opportunity for each of the traditions represented to demonstrate its hospitality. Embrace the differences and aim to make the occasion happy, memorable and good *fun* for everyone. Most cultures know how to enjoy themselves!

The bride and groom may each find a way to honour the other's culture or faith in front of the gathering, and this might be in the readings or music, in the clothing, or a special present, or at the meal. Be sure that whatever it is, it will be appreciated. If it is a surprise gesture, that would be charming too.

When one partner converts

Some couples take a further step, when one of them converts to the faith of the other. Most religions do not insist on this, but it comes from the wishes of the couple themselves. One such couple comprises Kirsty, who comes from a committed Christian family, and Morris, who is Jewish. Kirsty decided to convert to Judaism and undertook a rigorous period of study.

She explains: 'I didn't really know much about Judaism initially. And I didn't realise that Morris was Jewish when I first met him five years ago. It was a gradual process. Morris would explain about the festivals he was celebrating and the special foods for each one. I was intrigued. When we first thought of getting married, we believed conversion would be difficult and into the strictly orthodox Jewish tradition it is at least a four-year process.

'We thought of marrying in a registry office but then Morris's brother, who is a rabbi in Canada, made me realise that I could convert in the more conservative tradition. It was entirely my decision.

'My mother's faith is very important to her and she plays a part in the life of a major cathedral. Even so, although she had some mixed feelings, she was in favour of my converting. She needed to know that I wouldn't be an outsider.

'There was a lot of preparation and the hard work lasted for more than a year, but I found it fascinating. The whole experience was fantastic and very spiritually uplifting, particularly the final rite, *Mikveh*, which is an immersion, rather like a baptism, which took place just three weeks before our wedding. And that was a very special day. My new family were so proud of me and my achievement.'

At their wedding, Kirsty's Christian family and friends were welcomed and were offered an elegant booklet written by Morris's father explaining the ceremony, its customs and symbolism. It was a gesture that was much appreciated by all who attended.

Celebratory tale: Gary and Rosario

When Gary and Rosario decided to marry, they had very little income. He was a graphic designer just a year out of college and Rosario, who comes from northern Spain, was not at that time able to work here. A large celebration looked unlikely.

Even so, Rosario wanted a church wedding and, as Gary is an atheist, went to see her priest to discuss how this might be done. She learned that special dispensation was required and that this might take up to two years. The pair did not want to wait that long and so opted for a civil ceremony at Chelsea Register Office. Gary's family and all his friends attended, and afterwards they had an informal get-together in the couple's flat. On the following day, Gary's close family and his best man flew with the newly-weds to Spain, where Rosario's family had planned a traditional Spanish reception. It helped that Rosario's step-father was in catering and had already offered to throw the party for them in the function rooms of a local restaurant. Gary and Rosario wore their wedding clothes and guests arrived with their presents.

Gary says: 'The Spanish are immensely practical. They not only gave us envelopes of money as presents, but they also paid for their own meals. I found this embarrassing at first but it's the norm there. There were no speeches, but at any point guests could get up and toast the bride and groom. And they certainly did. The party lasted all day and well into the night!'

Gary's advice:

Try to integrate and learn the language if you can. My life has been so enriched by my marriage. My mother has come to enjoy the Spanish lifestyle too. As for a mixed culture wedding, it may be different from what you expect, but hey, it's a celebration, relax, enjoy it!

8 Budget & green weddings

More dash than cash

There are many people who do not have a large budget for their wedding, or who simply do not wish to spend a large amount in this way. This does not imply that their wedding has any less meaning, nor does it have to lack style. In fact, by looking at ways to reduce the budget, you may well be more imaginative, and create a highly individual event.

Stationery

For a smaller, more intimate event, there's no reason why you should not handwrite the invitations. It becomes much more personal. You could make the invitation a letter:

Hatch Cottage
Stratford-upon-Avon.
12th March 2007

Dear Dominic

Charlie and I are to be married at All Saints Parish Church near Burford on Saturday, 6th May at 11 a.m. We are inviting only a small number of our closest family and friends to attend, and we would both love it if you would join us. It would help make this day even more special. Please do let us know if you can come. We will be having a wedding breakfast at The Cross Hands afterwards.

With best wishes,
Grace

Or:

The Holly Lodge
Burford
18th March 2007

Dear Andrew and Elizabeth,

Our daughter Grace is marrying Charles Attwood at All Saints Parish Church near Burford on Saturday, 6th May at 11 a.m. They have decided that they wish for a very intimate wedding with just our closest family and friends attending. You have been such good friends to our family for so many years and Grace has always been so fond of you both. We would all be truly delighted if you would join us on this special occasion. We will be having a wedding breakfast at The Cross Hands afterwards.

Please do let us know if you are able to come.

Yours sincerely,

Henry and Clara Graham

You could just as easily choose attractive postcards and handwrite the usual formula (see page 82). Alternatively, you could create an invitation on your computer or find a friend who enjoys computer design. You could personalise the invitation to each guest. Remember that some people like to prop up their invitations, so you may wish to use a card heavy enough to allow this. Send the invitations early and use second-class stamps.

You can be equally creative about the service sheets and the place names for a reception meal.

Dressing up

There was a time when many people made their own clothes, or knew someone who was gifted with a sewing-machine and hand-finishing. Such people still exist and this may prove an economical way to go, particularly if you are not a stock size. It also has the advantage of allowing you not only to find a fabric you love, but also to select precisely both the style and the trimmings.

Certain charity shops now have specialist bridal departments. Oxfam, for instance, maintains that 95 per cent of the hundreds of gowns it sells each week are brand new, as they are ends of ranges or have been worn on the catwalk. They also have veils, tiaras and shoes. Some even offer clothes for the bridegroom and mother of the bride. The average price of a dress – a few hundred pounds – will provide 100 people with clean water, build two toilets, train one midwife or feed a family for a month.

You can also look on shopping websites such as Ebay, but the dresses will probably have been worn at least once. However, this is a wonderful way to find a vintage dress from the 20s or 30s or whatever is your dream style. You can also scour flea markets and antique clothing shops.

For men, there's the option to hire, or at the very least to buy a suit that can be worn again after the service.

For bridesmaids and other attendants, there is a wonderful array on the high street. These may not be designated as bridal clothes, but with a few extras they can be made to look wonderfully festive. You can even take a basic frock in a suitable fabric and add beading, embroidery or trimmings yourself.

Keep your hair simple – although a good cut is a worthwhile investment – or ask a friend or relative to help you dress it. Rather than expensive veils or tiaras, use ribbons and fresh flowers: they cost little but look enchanting.

Flowers and decorations

There are a number of suggestions in the following section on making your wedding greener that are also cost effective. Make your own floral decorations, or ask an artistic friend or relative to help. Use garden or wild flowers tied with ribbons or strips of lace in the spring and summer; find leaves, twigs, herbs and foliage for the autumn and berries and seedpods in the winter. Be creative about table decorations: candles, sea drift, shells, beads, moss and bark and trailing ivy in tumbled arrangements can look marvellous.

Reception venues

Heritage venues, luxury hotels and large marquees are hugely expensive. Pretty village halls and church halls can have every bit as much atmosphere. So can local cafes, tearooms and garden centres (where there is often a cafe area). However for these latter options you will have to consider their licensed status. If anyone in the family belongs to a sports club or local association, ask them to see if the club rooms or pavilions are available. Sometimes local pubs have garden rooms and restaurants and wine bars have separate rooms they can section off.

Food and wines

In many Mediterranean countries, reception guests either bring or pay for their own celebratory meal. They appreciate that it is an expensive element of the celebration.

- If the wedding service is in the morning, consider a wedding 'brunch': scrambled eggs decorated with mini strips of smoked salmon, bacon wrapped around mushrooms or around spears of asparagus if it is in season and available cheaply locally.
- If the wedding is in the early afternoon, why not hold a tea? Have elegant little sandwiches, scones with masses of jam and cream, small iced cakes.
- French champagne is a matter purely of tradition. There are some equally fine sparkling wines from other countries, made by the same method. Alternatively consider a prosecco,

the light dry sparkling wine from Italy, which is often relatively inexpensive but totally delicious.

- If you are going for a full dinner meal, ask a friend or relative to make the wines part of your wedding present. Ensure that everyone in the party toasts this kind sponsor.

Cakes

Most families will know someone who can bake a good cake, and who would be flattered to be asked. It doesn't have to be an elaborate tiered affair. Single layer cakes taste every bit as good! By all means offer to pay for the ingredients and to find decorations. A few tiny flowers and pretty ribbon can be charming.

Photography and videography

In both instances, you could approach a local college with a photography and film school and ask the tutors to recommend students to undertake your wedding as a project. Discuss what you can afford. They will probably put their hearts and souls into the job for a very modest rate! Explain the kind of approach you would like. If you would prefer something more traditional than avant garde, say so!

Ask all your guests to bring digital cameras and video cameras, and to edit their shots themselves. Make a special request that they load their best efforts on to a computer programme such as Photobox. They will need a password, but then everyone will be able to view the combined result.

Making your wedding greener

If you are worried about the environment and have concerns about human wastefulness – as indeed we all should – you can add touches that will make your wedding more environmentally friendly. There are now specialist planners of green weddings as well as several good websites offering advice, and there are even companies offering green wedding lists.

You can choose to have your wedding invitations, reply cards and order-of-service sheets printed using vegetable-based inks, on paper that is chlorine-free, with the pulp from European forests managed for sustainability. Most good quality printers and stationers will be able to source this for you. Alternatively, you can avoid paper, stamps and postal transportation altogether and send your invitations by email. You can also keep everyone up to date with your own wedding website.

Men's outfits can always be hired. However, brides sometimes baulk at the idea of hiring a wedding dress that has been worn by others. Consider the charity shop option mentioned under the budget wedding section or instead explore the family attics for grandmother's wedding dress, or search in vintage/antique clothes shops for dresses that can be revamped. Often the fabrics are unusual and gorgeous, and the garments are beautifully made. Brides may wish to wear natural cosmetics that have not been tested on animals and contain only plant extracts.

Consider family heirlooms as wedding rings or have them made from recycled gold. If you're buying a diamond, check with your jeweller that it is certified by the Kimberley Process – thus avoiding purchasing stones from conflict zones. Or even buy a fake diamond or recycle an old one.

Other ideas:

- Ask your guests not to throw confetti but instead to toss dried or fresh rose petals (depending on season and availability) or dried lavender seeds. It's a very charming and aromatic solution! Another alternative is to offer guests baskets of birdseed to throw.
- Use a local photographer, so there's no transport involved. Use a local videographer or filmmaker too. The latest film cameras don't require film but record on to film 'sticks', which go straight on to a computer hard drive, so cutting waste. Ask the

photographer to set up a picture site online, and ask the video-grapher to create a video 'stream' so there's no requirement for shipping, DVDs or postage.

Have a green reception

Hold your reception party close to or in the same place as the ceremony, so the bridal party and guests can walk between the two venues. If this is not possible and the venues are some distance away, the bride and groom could consider a tandem or a rickshaw. If walking between the venues is not possible, consider hiring a coach or bus for your guests, so there is only one vehicle involved, instead of many.

If possible, choose a venue that has plenty of accommodation so all your guests can stay on site. Try to find a venue that has a heritage handle, or is run by not-for-profit organisations or charities, or where it is a community project, such as a museum, public gallery and village hall. One couple who hold strong ethical principles held their wedding in a yoga retreat.

If you use a marquee company, ask them if they offset their CO2 emissions or you can do it on their behalf (you could do this as well for all your guests' travel to your celebrations). Several websites, such as www.climatecare.org.uk, can help you do this.

The lighting and music can often use a lot of electricity. The solution is to have a live band instead and use LED lighting and fairy lights, and even soy wax candles to create a romantic mood. Instead of unethical fireworks, choose Chinese flying lanterns to send your wishes into the sky, creating a magical finale to the day.

You can make your own floral decorations, or find an artistic family member or friend to do it for you.

- Choose seasonal flowers.
- Pick garden flowers for the bridal bouquet, add wild grasses and tie with handfuls of raffia or old lace.
- If it is an autumn or winter wedding, arrange to dry flowers

and leaves. Roses can be hung, copper beech leaves can be stood in glycerine and so on. You can also use herbs, berries, leaves and twigs, evergreens and fruits. Otherwise, look for winter jasmine. Maybe a neighbour has some, and may well be honoured to give flowers for the bride.

- Use tangled piles of ivy and trailing plants, cones, pretty pebbles, beads, raffia and coloured string to decorate reception tables, or use potted lilies or orchids that have a life and give pleasure to other people after the event. You may like to ask a bridesmaid or usher to arrange for them to be taken to an old people's home or hospice afterwards.

If you do use a florist, ask them where their flowers come from and request local first, or fair-trade and organic if possible. Ask them if they compost their green waste and recycle their packaging.

Ask whoever is doing the catering to ensure that all the food is from local suppliers, or if that's not possible, then at least British. Try to source food that is 100% organic as well, although not if that means transportation from abroad. It's more important ecologically that the food is grown locally. The same goes for drinks: select British champagnes and wines, or consider fine British cider and fruit wines as alternatives. And, of course, you can specify that your cake is made with organic and fair-trade ingredients.

Eco-presents

Bridegrooms may wish to give eco-presents to the bridesmaids, such as organic rosewater or other natural perfumes. If you have time, you can make green wedding favours yourself: little pots of jam, tiny living plants in containers to put at each place setting, local honeycomb, or soy wax candles – the list is endless, but make it personal.

If you think your relatives and friends are not aware of your green leanings, give them a wedding list to choose presents from, ensuring that you have specified all the relevant websites and stores.

- There are many companies now offering organic fair-trade products, including cotton bed linens and towels.
- There are several ranges of ethically produced goods, such as mats and mattresses made from organic coir, from areas where no insecticides and pesticides have been used.
- Opt for eco kettles and energy efficient appliances.
- Request handmade pottery and craftsman-made gifts, or commission an heirloom of the future from a master craftsman and have your guests contribute to it instead of opting for loads of smaller gifts. It is truly a lifetime's reminder of a very special moment.
- There are charity gift lists for couples who already have everything. A charity wedding list service is where guests can donate money in the couple's name which will go to a charity of their choice. Some are organised so that your friends and relations can buy you a well in the Sudan or a herd of goats in Southern Africa.

Finally, plan a honeymoon in the UK or choose one of the ethical travel companies if you long to go abroad. Flying is one of the fastest-growing causes of global warming. If you fly, you can elect to offset those carbon emissions by investing in carbon-reducing projects. Remember too that flying directly to your destination is preferable to stop-overs since it is taking off and landing that causes the highest emissions.

A wedding present for the earth

Plant a tree somewhere special in honour of your wedding and visit it on special anniversaries. Check with the local parish council; they will advise you where trees are needed.

When the tree is large enough, carve your initials, and show your children where those initials are so they too can find them on special occasions – maybe on their own wedding days.

Green - and budget conscious - stags and hens

Rosie Ames, founder of Green Union, a green weddings organiser based in Devon, has the following advice for pre-wedding celebrations:

If you're considering a bit of last-minute bonding with your nearest and dearest, why not continue with the health and beauty regime? The great outdoors is a good place to start with camping, walking, surfing and sailing. A cosy B&B with pampering built in for the not so active, or take mums away to a spa. Learn to make something for the wedding on a residential course – your wedding bouquet, a piece of jewellery for your bridesmaids, or carve a piece of wood or a stone sculpture. Go fishing and have a barbeque on the beach, but whatever it is, stay in the UK, take the train, cycle or walk.

Celebratory tale: Brandon and Marie-Louise

Marie-Louise, an actress living in Paris, and Brandon, a New York filmmaker, decided to marry in Cornwall where Marie-Louise's parents lived. Marie-Louise is a practising Catholic; Brandon is secular. As an American, he needed a special visa to marry in the UK; neither were resident in Cornwall.

The pair didn't create a budget, but trusted one another to spend as little as possible. Of great importance was having a 'low stress' wedding. Brandon explains: 'This means you don't want a huge guest list, huge hotel, huge cake . . . huge anything. Low stress keeps everything to a manageable size. We sought to give our wedding meaning and style – but inexpensively.'

In the event, their biggest expense was Brandon's visa and their flights to the UK. Another priority was the fare from London of Father George, a Franciscan priest whom they knew well, as it was important to them that he conducted the ceremony.

They elected to be married in the Roman Catholic chapel at

Lanherne in St Mawgan-in-Pydar, an old country house, now a Franciscan monastery and convent, which Marie-Louise had known since childhood. First, they quickly undertook their marriage preparation with Marie-Louise's local priest in Paris, and ensured that all necessary paperwork was sent to the diocese of Plymouth. As non-residents, they were required to stay in Cornwall – with Marie-Louise's parents – for seven nights prior to the ceremony, registering their intention to marry with the Cornish local authority.

It was a small wedding, just 30 family and friends. The couple didn't spend on formal invitations but handwrote their invitations on ivory calling cards, bought from a Paris papeterie.

Marie-Louise had wanted an antique wedding dress from the 30s or 40s – a glamorous starlet gown – and found one on Ebay. Unfortunately it was lost in the post so, with only days to go, and on tour in Greece, she miraculously found a lovely ivory silk gown in Athens, in similar 30s style but new and in the sales. She added traditionally made silver sandals and handmade silver-and-pearl earrings and a necklace from an artist in Naplion, on the Greek coast, famous for its pearls.

Marie-Louise didn't want a veil, but instead chose to wear flowers and ribbons. 'My mother dressed my hair, which was a special moment of ritual for us both. My mother's family is Irish, and I wanted to keep one of their traditions – historically brides wore blue in Ireland – so I chose cornflower blue and ivory ribbons, with white roses. I used the same ribbons from a little Cornish haberdashery to make wedding favours.'

The day before the wedding she realised that she hadn't arranged her bouquet, beyond wanting a posy of white roses and myrtle, but the owner of a local garden centre was also a florist and made it for her. 'Nor did I toss the posy at the end of the day, as is traditional. It was so beautiful that I kept it throughout our honeymoon, throwing it as a ritual into the ocean on the last day.'

Marie-Louise's parents helped with the reception. The couple were opposed to a formal, sit-down affair so, as the wedding was in the afternoon, they had a tea party in the Village Stores and Post Office, which had a tearoom and garden, a minute's walk from the chapel. Marie-Louise says: 'It was the owners' first wedding reception, and they were wonderful. They even erected a gazebo in case of poor weather. We had a Cornish cream tea, smoked salmon sandwiches and fruit desserts; we were especially happy that all produce was local. A local woman made us a pretty one-tier cake.'

Originally, Brandon hadn't wanted to marry in a church of any kind, while a secular wedding was unthinkable for Marie-Louise. Their solution was to have a second ceremony. After the reception, at the end of the day, they had their own ritual, an exchange of personal vows, on the clifftops nearby.

Brandon explains:

I had the idea of this personal exchange and it proved a real highlight. Any official marriage ceremony – civic or church – has its own format. We felt that we had more to say. I kept one small religious tradition myself. After my personal vow, I placed a small glass in a velvet bag on the ground and stomped on it. This is a Jewish tradition. I have always liked this remembrance of the destruction of the second temple. I've kept the bag and broken glass as a keepsake.

9 Weddings abroad

A growing trend has been to hold the wedding overseas. This may be because of family ties and associations with the country concerned, or because the couple plans to live there, or it could just be the sheer glamour of the idea. It can also be an ideal solution for couples who have family dilemmas that don't lend themselves to a traditional happy gathering, perhaps where parents are divorced acrimoniously, or even where the family does not approve of the wedding.

Some of the large travel companies offer various kinds of wedding 'packages', from a simple civil ceremony and wedding breakfast for a small group to a more expensive, fairly elaborate ceremony and reception. If you are considering this option, take a close look at precisely what is – and what is not – included in the package. You may wish to follow David and Marisa's advice (see Celebratory Tale on page 79) and visit the venue beforehand.

There are a number of smaller companies that offer a bespoke service, often specialising in weddings in one particular country or part of the world. They are likely to pay more attention to detail and have in-depth knowledge about the country you have chosen. Of course, you can organise the wedding abroad yourself but, if you wish to do this, allow plenty of preparation time.

There can be advantages to holding your wedding in another country. You can choose a special and romantic place that has guaranteed good weather in certain seasons and you can extend your stay so that it becomes your honeymoon as well. A wedding abroad may even be better value because, despite the flights and hotel accommodation, you probably won't be facing the enormous costs of a large reception, which often takes the lion's share of the wedding budget.

There can be one major disadvantage: it is likely to be a smaller wedding. Not all friends or family members will be able to take the time away, because they have children at school or business commitments, or they may simply be unable to afford the trip.

The further challenge is the amount of preparation, in terms of documentation, you may face.

Legal requirements

Even within the EU, and certainly outside of it, the legal requirements differ enormously. The first step therefore is to contact the London-based embassy, consulate or high commission of the country in which you wish to be married. They will be able to advise you about their procedures, and all the documentation you will require. If your spouse-to-be is a resident of the proposed country, he or she will also have to register their desire to marry in the equivalent of their local town hall or registry office. If they are an ex-pat or have temporary residency abroad, they will need to go to the nearest British embassy to request information.

Some countries have a minimum residency requirement, which means that both the bride and the bridegroom will have to stay in the country concerned for some time prior to the wedding. This can range from 40 days for countries such as France to three days for Greece. However, some countries, Hawaii for example and other parts of the USA, require no residency period at all.

Documentation

There are wide variations in the documentation that different countries require. The most usual requirements include:

- UK long form birth certificates
- UK certificates of No Impediment or Nulla Ostas. This is proof

that you are free to marry. If this is required, it can usually be obtained from your local registry office in the UK.

- UK divorce documents
- UK passports
- A UK change of name deed poll.

All the British documents you require for use overseas must also be subject to 'legalisation', that is, the official confirmation that a signature, seal or stamp appearing on the document is genuine. Again, check with the embassy, consulate or high commission which documents require legalisation and in some instances, translation as well. The Foreign and Commonwealth Office will undertake the legalisation process – there is a fee per document – and this can be done by either taking the documents to their public counter, or sending them by post. If you make a postal application, you should send the documents by recorded or special delivery and you should allow at least four weeks' processing time. For more information, check the website: www.fco.gov.uk.

The embassy, consulate or high commission can advise about their requirement for the translation of your documents.

Making sure the marriage is recognised in the UK

Your marriage will be recognised in the UK as long as it has complied with the laws of the country in which the ceremony was held. At the same time, it should be noted that the marriage cannot be registered here. There is no legal requirement for you to do so, but if you wish for a record to be kept in the UK of your marriage, you can have your marriage documents deposited at the General Register Office (GRO). You can then apply to the GRO for certified copies of your marriage certificate at any time. However, marriage certificates issued in a Commonwealth country or Overseas Territory cannot be placed with the GRO. If you live overseas, you can apply for this service through the nearest British Consulate. If you are resident in the UK you should apply via the Foreign and Commonwealth Office.

Cautionary tale: Christa

Christa Valsin was an events organiser for BT before becoming a wedding planner. Her company, *C'est Deux*, specialises in overseas weddings, mainly in France where the list of legal requirements includes a minimum of 40 days' residency prior to the wedding and a compulsory medical examination for both bride and bridegroom. A prenuptial certificate of good health must be issued by a medical doctor less than two months before the date of the marriage, and this will cover serological tests for syphilis, irregular antibodies, rubella and toxoplasmosis. On rare occasions this will delay or jeopardise your wedding.

She gives this advice: 'I speak fluent French and I'm experienced in organising weddings throughout France, yet it is not always easy even for me. You must be prepared for completely different attitudes in other cultures. Couples often don't realise how long it takes to sort out the documentation, lodge it along with the relevant applications in time, and to sort out the medicals and the residency. It can take up to three trips to arrange all of this. And if there is a backlog of paperwork, which happens in the more popular parts of France such as in the south, the officials simply don't get it done in time!'

Christa's advice:

There is an alternative, particularly when the couple are both from the UK and seeking a civil wedding, rather than a religious service. I would suggest that the couple has a civil marriage ceremony in their local registry office in the UK, then a blessing ceremony in their country of choice. This way, you can still have your dream wedding in a chateau or in a vineyard, but you cut out all the legal headaches, all the nightmares of paperwork.

Church weddings

In addition to the civil legalities, a church wedding overseas will require further advance preparation involving the church authorities. You will need to gain the necessary permission, and then make your arrangements with the priest of the chosen church. Some faiths, including the Catholic tradition, require marriage preparation before the service and this must be fitted into your time schedule, although possibly you could arrange to undertake this during your period of residence.

Translation

As mentioned previously, some countries require the translation of your documentation. You, on the other hand may need a translation of the service, whether a civil ceremony or a church service. Unless you are fluent in the language of the country in which you are marrying, it may be wise to obtain the services of a good translator.

Venues

In some countries, such as Australia, Canada, New Zealand and South Africa, you can hold a wedding in just about any location. In the US you can hold your ceremony on a mountain, a beach or even underwater swimming with dolphins if you so wish. In other countries, the practice is much the same as here: there are approved venues for ceremonies and a much wider choice for the parties afterwards.

Most couples marrying abroad wish to incorporate some of the local colour, perhaps with local food and flowers for the reception. Others like to import at least a few of their own traditions, perhaps taking the wedding cake with them or choosing flowers, music or readings that have particular meaning for them and their families. By and large, wherever you are, people will try to make it a special day for a bride.

Passport validity

We have looked at passports under the section on page 15, but it is worth repeating that it is wise to check that everyone in the party has a passport that will be valid at the time. Some countries are strict about denying entry to people whose passports are in the last few months before expiry. Again, check with the country's embassy, consulate or high commission here about their passport regulations and the need for any other kind of visa.

Vaccinations and other health precautions

If you are travelling outside of Western Europe, check to see if any vaccinations are required. Some vaccines, such as those for malaria, should be taken at least eight weeks before departure. It may be a good idea to have all inoculations done well in advance just in case someone in the party reacts to them.

Other necessary precautions include a good diarrhoea remedy, appropriate insect repellents and the right level of sun block.

Celebratory Tale: Marisa and David

Marisa and David had been together for 10 years and very much wanted to get married. Their dilemma was that Marisa's parents were divorced and her father had remarried, and she knew that a family gathering would be uncomfortable. They had already decided to have a civil ceremony since neither held strong religious beliefs, but they knew that wherever they decided to hold the wedding, the family problem would remain and they didn't want to create anxiety or cause arguments. In the event, they created the wedding they wanted, surrounded by close friends, that was both inexpensive and stress-free.

The solution came through a brochure for ski holidays that also contained wedding options, from simple to elaborate. They selected a basic wedding package for a winter wedding in Zell am See, an Austrian resort, mainly because Austria has a very short residency requirement. However, Marisa decided she needed to connect with the arrangements and the place beforehand, so they visited Zell am See during the previous summer.

She says: 'Zell is absolutely beautiful, set on a lake. We could not have chosen better. We met the hotel owners, who proved to be fantastic – immensely kind – and allowed us to deal with them directly on the more detailed arrangements, rather than via the holiday company.

'There was a party of eleven of us in all. David and I paid for the best man and his family's accommodation but not fares, because he chose to drive over, and we also paid for our two witnesses, although not for their partners. Everyone paid for their own ski equipment,' Marisa explains.

Hunting for her wedding dress, Marisa found the simple, elegant style she was looking for and was delighted when she realised that it was actually designated as a bridesmaid's dress, at about a tenth of the cost. With it came a chiffon jacket, ideal for the evening dinner. She found her shoes in a sale. For the morning ceremony, she discovered a lace coat on the seconds rail of a stand at a wedding show. 'It needed a good wash but otherwise it was just right. I still have it and plan to give it to my daughter to play at dressing up. If you shop around, you just don't have to buy into this big wedding thing!'

David bought a suit that he could wear again. One of the witnesses was an army officer so wore his dress uniform. Marisa decided to take the cake from England, made as a gift by a friend, and she decorated it herself in the hotel's kitchens. Meanwhile, the hotel arranged her flowers, her only stipulation being that she wanted iris and ivy because they were her mother's and maternal grandmother's names.

Marisa says:

My bouquet was beautiful, hand-tied with pearls, as were the roses for the gentlemen's buttonholes. The hotel also organised the photographer, who took us down to the lake for our photographs. He brought us our album the next day. It was all so relaxed, even the civil service. Afterwards we drank mulled wine and had a light lunch at the hotel garden, then changed into jeans to walk around the lake. We dressed up again for the evening dinner. Then we all settled down to play a murder mystery game, drinking good wine and wondering whodunnit. It was totally without stress. And we still had three days' skiing left!

10 Invitations

The first place to start is the guest list. This can be a challenge as you juggle with the numbers of family members of both bride and bridegroom, family friends, friends of the couple, and people who are important to the family such as business associates, community leaders and so on.

Sometimes the list can be split between those invited to attend the ceremony (and the party afterwards) and those invited to attend just the reception. If the reception event will be in the evening, you may also have decisions to make about whether to invite families with babies and young children. Also be aware that however carefully you have chosen the date, there will be a number of people who will not be able to attend. Maybe they will be away on holiday or at an important business conference. Therefore allow for at least 10 to 15 per cent to decline your invitation. You can therefore safely prepare a reserve list!

The usual form is to send out invitations about six weeks before the event. However, if the wedding is being held in the summer holiday period or just before Christmas, when diaries become full very quickly, you may wish to send them out earlier or send out a 'save the date' card (see page 13).

Wording

There's a lot to be said for the old-fashioned formula: it contains all the necessary information: the host, the event, the venue, date and time, and usually some indication of how to dress. Nowadays when so many families experience divorce and remarriage, or it is a second marriage for one or both of the couple, there are subtle variations in wording.

For the larger wedding, the usual form is a formal printed invitation and the traditional wording is:

Mr and Mrs Robert Croft
request the pleasure of your company
at the marriage of their daughter
Helen
to
Mr Jules Raymond
at St Barnabas Church, Worthing
on Saturday 10th May, 2007
at 2.30 p.m.

and afterwards at
The Grange Hotel, Brighton

RSVP
1 Windsor Road
Worthing

RSVP is after the French, *repondez-vous s'il vous plait*, literally meaning 'Respond, if you please.'

If the mother and father of the bride are divorced and – in this case – Mrs Croft has not remarried, the first line can read: Mr Robert Croft and Mrs Jane Croft. If Mrs Croft has remarried and become Mrs Charles Black, the first line can read: Mr Robert Croft and Mrs Charles Black.

If Mrs Charles Black is hosting the wedding with her new husband, the first lines would read: Mr and Mrs Charles Black request the pleasure of your company for the marriage of Helen.

Where the marriage is between divorced people or older people, when their parents are no longer alive, the wedding invitation would be:

> *Miss Helen Croft and Mr Jules Raymond*
> *request the pleasure of your company*
> *at their marriage*

or, in the case of divorcees who may be having a civil ceremony, followed by a church blessing:

> *Mrs Jane Croft and Mr Charles Black*
> *request the pleasure of your company*
> *at a blessing of their marriage*

It is usual to show who is included in the invitation. One way is to write the names in the top right-hand corner. The alternative is to have the guests' names handwritten in the body of the invitation. In this instance, the second line would read 'request the pleasure of the company of', followed by a space for the guests' names. If budget allows on this kind of bespoke invitation, you may wish to commission a calligrapher to write in the names.

You can also do this pleasant task yourself, in which case the names should be written in ink, not biro. Try using a calligraphy pen or one with an 'italic' nib to add style to your writing. The usual greeting for children under 15 is by forename only. The guest line might read: Mr and Mrs Graham, Simon and Jessica.

Titles, including military and police ranks, are used on formal invitations, including that of the bridegroom. It would be wise to check the customs of the particular regiment or police service. A good reference book on letter-writing or etiquette will list the correct forms of address for invitees, both for the card and the envelope.

Stationery

The time-honoured combination for formal printed invitations is black copperplate script on one side only of a white, ivory or cream card, with black script. Decoration is usually simple, perhaps with a 'deckle', fine gold or bevel edge.

It is customary that the card will be either stand alone, that is, a post-card, or it will be 'fly', a card with a fold on the left that stands upright, like a book. The card should be sufficiently stiff that it will stand on a mantelpiece for up to six months; the smartest invites are up to 600 grams in weight. Other advice includes:

- Leave plenty of space around the words to avoid the corporate look.
- Similarly, avoid rounded corners and bright edging.
- Engraving can be expensive; use flat instead, but preferably not thermographic printing.
- Ensure that the typeface is legible. This is important for the response address and postcode.
- It is now usual to enclose a flat-printed reply card – this should be stamped and self-addressed.

You can consider having your menu cards and place cards for the reception in a matching style.

Most faiths have invitations on much the same lines. One charming addition is seen on Parsee wedding invitations. The last lines will often be the blessings of grandparents who have died and the compliments of aunts, brothers and sisters.

Formal invitations to the reception only

Several couples decide to have a small service, inviting just family and a few close friends, but want to follow it with a much larger reception. In this case, it's a good idea to have separate invitations printed for people you would like to attend the post-wedding celebrations. The form of words for this kind of invitation might be:

Mr and Mrs Hadrian Wall
invite
... (names by hand) ...
to attend the post-wedding celebrations of
their daughter, Angela and Mr Henry Higgins
at
Wadhams Golf & Country Club, Stevenage
On Saturday 12th December, 2007
From 6 p.m.

Dancing from 7 p.m. Carriages at 1 a.m.

Dress

It is wise – and courteous – to let people know what's expected of them. If morning suits and top hats will be worn, tell male guests in a little handwritten note. ('By the way, the majority of our gentlemen guests will be wearing morning suits.') If the event requires black tie, that is, a dinner jacket, either include it on the invitation or again send a separate note.

Many women wear hats to weddings. If the reception requires a change into evening dress, do warn your guests and let them know where there will be changing facilities.

'Decorations may be worn' is a good way of letting people know that the event is very formal.

Some London gentlemen's clubs insist that male guests wear jackets and ties, as do the messes of the military on formal occasions. It's wise not to assume that your family, friends and colleagues will automatically know the form. When in doubt, tell them!

Nowadays, 'dress casual' means just that, and you can expect a wide interpretation, although most people make a gesture towards glamour for a wedding.

Practicalities

The best invitations cover all the information the guests will need. Necessary information might include:

- travel directions. If people are strangers to the area, they will welcome directions. Check if the reception venue already has directions tested and written out or at least a local map
- car parking availability
- names of local hotels and guest houses if people are likely to want to stay over
- any transport that the hosts will be providing such as a coach between the church and the reception
- any crèche or babysitting arrangements for guests with small children
- notes about wheelchair access for anyone who may require it.

With so many people turning vegetarian or coping with food intolerances, you may wish to add a request for information to help with your catering. See the reply card below.

Reply cards

People really are very sloppy about answering invitations these days. One encouragement may be to enclose a small card, self-addressed and stamped for replies.

You could check other requirements at the same time, for instance: whether they require vegetarian or other special dietary considerations, crèche facilities or disabled car parking. For example:

Guests' names: ....

I/We are able/not able to attend Mike and Angie's wedding ceremony on 18th March

I/We are able/not able to attend the reception party at the Bell Hotel afterwards

I/We require:

> *Vegetarian food (number of people)* ....
> *Other diet requirement* ....
> *Crèche facility (number and ages)* ......
> *A disabled space* ....

Please help us by returning the card as soon as possible to Angie in the envelope provided!

Less Formal Weddings

You may not need invitations printed by a stationer for smaller, more private weddings. You can design your own on a computer and email them to some friends and relatives, and print off small numbers for anyone who would find that more appropriate. Handwritten invitations are always acceptable, but use ink rather than a biro. You can either use a wording similar to the formal invitations or you can turn it into a short letter:

> 56 Maryland Lane
> St Columb, Cornwall TR7
> 29th August, 2007

> Dear Eileen and Paul,
> Jamie and I are to be married at St Petroc Parish Church on Saturday 2nd October at 12 noon. We are inviting only a small number of our closest friends to attend, and we both very much hope that you will be there. Please do let us know if you are able to

come. We will be having a wedding breakfast at the Watergate Bay Hotel, near Newquay, afterwards.

It will be an informal wedding but we hope that our gentle-men guests will wear jackets and ties, and the ladies are very wel-come to sport a hat if they want to! There is plenty of parking near the church in the village, and we suggest that our guests use the public car park at Watergate Bay. Do let me know if either of you would like a vegetarian meal.

With best wishes,

Yours sincerely,

Helen

The same courtesies regarding information for guests will apply, as for a more formal wedding. They will need to know how to reach the venues, how formally or informally they should dress, where to park, and that they should inform you of any dietary needs.

11 Pre- and post-wedding celebrations

Pre-wedding parties

Within living memory, the stag night was organised by the best man on the eve of the wedding when the bridegroom, along with his siblings and chums, celebrated his last night as a bachelor, usually with some form of alcoholic trial-by-fire. As equality of the sexes advanced so the bride and *her* siblings and chums decided that they would have a party or outing to acknowledge her last night without the responsibilities of marriage. This was often organised by the chief bridesmaid.

In some communities this is still the pattern. In others, pre-wedding parties have grown into a quite different form of celebration. Many couples live together before marriage and many of their friends do the same, so they opt for a joint pre-wedding party. Same-sex couples tend to do likewise. Usually these celebrations are held at least a week in advance of the wedding to avoid facing the big day with a sore head.

Some of these parties are extravagant affairs, with elaborate themes – circus, Caribbean, Moulin Rouge and so on – and are organised by professional events organisers.

Others decide that there will be enough partying and choose a special event. This can range from long weekends in European capital cities to an adventure sports trip, a day at the races or the dogs, or a meeting at Brands Hatch or Silverstone. Sometimes, the girls like to wallow in a health spa – and sometimes their partners like to join them!

If friends and family are coming long distances, often the bride and groom, either together or separately, want to spend time with them. They might therefore organise a short trip or a series of treats so they can all be together before the main celebration.

If you are planning a green wedding, there are further ideas in our green weddings chapter on page 66.

Cautionary Tale: Max

If you are considering a major pre-wedding event or trip, you should also give thought to the impact on the people you invite to join you. Usually, anyone accompanying the bridegroom – or bride – pays for him or herself. Now, this may be a one-off occasion in *your* life, but friends could be facing several weddings in a year.

Max found himself in just this situation. Two of his close friends from university and his cousin all got married within 12 months, and he was invited to join them on stag trips, one of which was five days' skiing in the US. This proved very expensive, and he simply couldn't spend so much on the wedding presents. The trips took up his entire year's holiday allowance and they weren't really the sort of treats that he would have chosen.

Max's advice:

Consider setting up a series of smaller events so budget-conscious friends can still join in your celebrations.

Honeymoons

Once again, there are huge variations, based less on tradition and more on the preferences of the couple. Some wish to get away from all the brouhaha of the wedding preparations as soon as possible, and relax together. Others will elect for a few nights away immediately after the wedding but plan a major honeymoon trip anything up to a year later.

If you are planning a honeymoon following the wedding celebrations, then consider the practicalities:

- Decide the kind of holiday you will both enjoy.
- You may find that some tour operators, hotels and holiday centres have special rooms or 'extras' for honeymooners such as flowers and champagne. Decide whether you wish for it to be known that you are on your honeymoon or whether you would rather be 'incognito'.
- If you are honeymooning abroad, decide whether the bride will change her name on her passport immediately or later. Check that both passports are valid for the trip (some countries will not accept passports if the expiry date is within six months). Allow time to obtain any necessary visas and, if you are going long-haul, check any requirements for vaccinations.
- Into the wedding preparation schedule, add, where necessary:
    - buying holiday insurance
    - ordering currency.
- Enlist the help of the best man and chief bridesmaid to ensure that luggage, tickets and going-away clothes are in the right places at the right time, along with the taxi or your other transport.
- Don't forget your camera!

12 Dressing up and taking care of yourself

The bride's dress

There is no bride on earth who doesn't want to look her most stunning on her wedding day. The selection of the outfit often therefore becomes a major undertaking.

Tastes vary according to age and culture, and the personality of the bride, but – style aside – there are elements that all brides may wish to consider when making their choice.

Many traditions favour white, which traditionally symbolises virginity and new beginnings. If, however, white kills your complexion, you may find oyster, which has delicate pink undertones, a gentle cream, palest beige or icy blue are better options. Be guided by your skin tone.

In fact, it was Queen Victoria who started the trend towards white dresses. There is currently a move away from white and pale colours to coloured and even patterned fabrics. This gives the opportunity for the groom to incorporate the same or a complementary fabric into his clothing.

Whatever the style, it is worth remembering that generations to come will be fascinated by the photographs. It may be fun now to have something vaguely shocking or extreme, but only the bride and bridegroom can decide whether they will relish their children and grandchildren falling about laughing at some stage in the future. Classic styles are timeless and this should be a timeless event.

In making your choice, remember that your dress will be seen from different angles and, during the service, it will be mainly a rear view.

Check to see that your dress looks as gorgeous from behind as in front. If you are going to have a train, make sure that it is detachable, which will be easier when you are sitting at the reception meal – and for the dancing later.

Try to find an outfit that doesn't crease unflatteringly in the first few hours. This is important because you will be photographed – officially and by friends – throughout the occasion and creases can show up badly. Ideally, the outfit should look uncrushed even after the bride has had to kneel, be seated in a vehicle and at the reception meal, and perhaps dance. The chances are that the bride will be hugged not only by her new husband but also by family and friends as well. It would be a shame to have an outfit that cannot withstand this – or is so formal or fragile that people are afraid to touch. The quality of the fabric is therefore one of the most important considerations. If necessary, have a slimmer silhouette, that is, a dress with less material in a high quality fabric so it hangs better and creases less, rather than acres of cheaper fabric that crushes. Be aware too that very shimmery fabrics may be difficult to photograph.

As soon as you have selected your dress – or the style if you are having it made – book an appointment with a fitter at a reputable underwear shop or the lingerie department in a large store. At the least, take her a drawing or photo of your gown. You may even want to take the gown itself. The fitter will help you find underwear that fits properly, and enhances the look of your outfit, without any ridges, strap outlines, or unsightly seams. You will probably wish for different underwear again for your honeymoon and this may be the right time to select that too. Even the smallest wisps of lace and satin ribbon need to be in the most flattering places!

If it is a winter wedding, find a pretty wrap or cape. Cold brides in photographs look – *cold*. Or, like the former Mrs Camilla Parker-Bowles at her wedding to HRH The Prince of Wales, opt for a matching coat and dress. You can always wear it to the opening night of the opera afterwards! Consider having a suitably bridal umbrella ready and available.

If you are a more mature bride, again follow the Duchess of

Cornwall's example and opt for elegance and sophistication, rather than trying to look like a young bride. Lace can be quite ageing – think of the late Queen Mother. Instead, opt for smooth sensual fabrics, such as silks, chiffons and crepes.

People will want to see and photograph the bride and therefore any veils, headdresses (also known as 'fascinators'), hats or hairstyles should not only flatter but also be away from the face.

Every woman looks better in a heel, unless she is very tall. The better the shoe, the better the construction and the more comfortable it is likely to be, both to walk in and stand for long periods of time. Both mules and slingbacks are very flattering.

Make-up

Style guru Patrick Swan, who has made up some of the world's most famous stars for photoshoots, offers the following advice:

- Start a skin regime several months in advance, to allow for peels to work and the skin to calm down properly. Have your final facial a week before the wedding; at the very latest, four days beforehand.
- It's tempting to use more make-up than normal because you are facing a camera. In fact, less is more! By all means add more mascara – up to three coats – but otherwise keep it fresh and light.
- Ensure that mascara is waterproof and, if you are likely to cry, don't use it on lower lashes. This may be a good tip to pass on to the bride's and the bridegroom's mothers too. Use black mascara unless you are very blonde, when black-brown may be more suitable.
- If you don't usually wear make-up, consider doing so. Practise beforehand or book a session with a make-up artist. Decide whether you wish to look entirely natural or whether you require a make-up that complements colours you are wearing.

- Whatever your choice, try not to look like someone different. It may be a mistake to try and create a period look, even if it is the theme of your wedding party, or a look that is over-stylised. This is the day when your make-up should simply be an enhancement of you.

- You are aiming for a glow, rather than a made-up look. If you are pale, use a blusher. If you flush red when excited, use a translucent powder rather than a heavy foundation to even out your skin tone. Gently define your brows, eyes and mouth.

- Gloss looks wonderful in photographs. Use gloss when you arrive and for the photographs and then stop worrying about it and go and enjoy your day. If you have a pale mouth, use a lip stain that will last all day. Just add gloss for the photographs.

- You don't have to change your make-up if you wear glasses, not even for photographs. But you may wish to consider your glasses. Why not have a pair of glamorous glasses for your wedding? Plastic frames tend to look younger than wire or frameless glasses – and, says Patrick, a little diamante never hurt anyone!

- Make it one of your chief bridesmaid's tasks to keep a supply of blusher, a lip gloss and a comb somewhere to hand for touching up before all those photos, or between the wedding service and the reception party.

- If you have terrible hair, pull it back and wear a hat or cover-up headdress. You don't want to spend your special day constantly checking that your hair is looking all right.

The attendants' outfits

If the bride is tall, slender and dark-haired, it will probably follow that what suits her may not suit bridesmaids or matrons of honour who are dumpy and red-haired. Having once been asked to wear yellow as a bridesmaid, which killed my olive skin, with a wide skirt that made me feel like a lampshade, I make a plea to all brides to be *kind* and adapt their ideas to bring out the best in their attendants.

Consider the height, proportions, hair and skin tones of each attendant. A group in complementary shades and variations of style, including necklines and skirt lengths, is preferable to a chorus line, none of whom look at ease. Consider the fabric. Very shiny fabrics or shot silk, where the colours change as people move, will give the photographer an immense challenge and may not look good in some of the pictures.

For adults, choose comfortable as well as pretty shoes that complement the outfits, remembering that not everyone can wear high heels for any length of time, and discuss headdresses and hairstyles well in advance.

Discuss outfits for child bridesmaids and pageboys with their mothers. Some children relish dressing up; others find it a trial. Look for styles that allow children to play at the reception party without it being a worry. Remember that children will often grow in spurts and that clothes bought or made six months in advance may not fit come the day. Look at high street stores as well as specialist wedding shops for children's outfits.

It's a nice touch if the bride arranges for the hairdressing of her bridesmaids as well as herself. As Patrick Swan points out, many small children are not good at having their hair done. He suggests that little girls look better with longer hair caught in a slide, rather than up or in a ponytail which probably won't last. The rule is: thinner the hair, thinner the slide; thicker the hair, thicker the slide. Avoid using any style with hairspray that makes hair look dry and wiry.

Most bridal attendants would like the option to adapt their outfits and wear them again on less formal occasions.

The bridegroom's outfit

In mainstream Christian tradition in the UK, it used to be that the bridegroom wore a tail suit and top hat at very smart weddings, or a lounge suit at more informal weddings. Other faiths have always incorporated wonderful colours and fabrics, and now this trend is being taken up.

'Toppers and tails' are still worn of course, but some men are opting for a good and even designer suit that can be worn again. Touches of colour – particularly if the bride is wearing a gorgeous fabric – can be added by way of ties and the linings of the jacket. Some men will also have a waistcoat made, not necessarily to be worn at the service, but to look dashing when they remove their jackets at the party afterwards.

Even if you are not planning to bring in the same fabrics as your bride, at least ensure that whatever you are wearing will complement her in the photographs. Often the bride's father, best man and ushers all co-ordinate their outfits with yours in colour and style. When in doubt, check with whoever is organising the wedding to see if this has been discussed.

If you are not good at creating a look, book in with the personal shopper in a good quality department store or – at the very least – find a friend or relative who will help you choose a shirt, tie, shoes and socks that are appropriate to your suit.

Other thoughts for the whole bridal party

- New shoes can sometimes pinch, and who wants to hobble on their wedding day? Wear your wedding shoes at home for at least a few hours before the wedding to break them in. Select shoes that have non-slip soles. Suggest to everyone else in the wedding party – bridegroom, best man, bridesmaids and parents – that they also 'break in' their new shoes.

- Book hair appointments early. The bride, her mother and attendants may wish for hairdressing on the morning of the wedding. The groom, bride's father and best man should consider booking a cut a few days to a week ahead to avoid that just-cropped look. Men with beards should consider a professional shave just before the event, and older men should request trims of bushy eyebrows, nose hair and around ears.

- This is the UK. We have rain on a regular basis. Brief one of the ushers to make sure there are umbrellas easily available for the entire wedding party throughout the day.
- It is useful if someone in the party carries some kind of kit for running repairs and other small emergencies. This may be the chief bridesmaid or maybe the bride's or groom's mother. Items for the kit might include safety pins, sticky tape (good for keeping up hems), needle and thread (in case important buttons come adrift), spare pairs of tights, tissues, make-up remover, stain remover and a headache remedy. A couple of plasters might also be useful for anyone whose shoes rub or who spears themselves with their buttonholes.

Slimming

Many brides will be tempted to put themselves into a diet and fitness regime before their wedding. By all means lose a few pounds by cutting out sweeties and fats, and by increasing your exercise. However, this is a time of high activity and there's a big element of stress. You will want to look gorgeous and glowing on your wedding day, not drained and wan. Refuse to take panic measures. Avoid drastic diets and instead opt for all the foods that will make you look wonderful: lots of fruits and vegetables, fish and lean meats, high quality fruit juices and smoothies with no additives, wholemeal breads and pasta. Cut out the coffee and alcohol for a few weeks and drink green or organic herbal teas instead. See a good nutritionist or herbalist to check if you require extra vitamins or minerals.

Organiser nerves

Even the most accomplished and experienced events organiser will feel the strain as the big day draws near. This has a positive aspect: it ensures that you check and double-check all the details. If you are too calm and laid back, the chances are that something important will be forgotten.

Even so, if the organiser – or the bride, or both – are becoming so stressed that they are losing sleep, a little healthcare is in order. You may like to consider trying herbal remedies first. Omega 3 and vitamin B complex will help. In Ayurveda, the traditional Indian system of health and wellbeing, there are remedies such as Valerian and Ashwagandha Formula that are recommended for disturbed sleep.

If you are becoming truly over-anxious, then a visit to your GP is in order. However, there should also come a time when you know that you have done as much as possible to make the wedding the very best it can be. That is the point at which you should relax, let it go . . . and prepare to enjoy yourself!

Bride and bridegroom nerves

Being the centre of attention, hoping you don't fluff your lines, and knowing you will be photographed all make for a very particular kind of pressure. Keep your diet fairly simple in the preceding days and keep any alcohol consumption within reasonable bounds. If you start feeling completely freaked, phone a good friend and talk it through. It should be one of the happiest days of your life, but you may start the day feeling sick with apprehension. Try to have breakfast, but make it something light that you find comforting.

There are a number of tried and true therapies, starting with deep gentle breathing. Nelson's Bach Rescue Remedy is wonderful for anxiety attacks and if you think you are likely to get into a real panic, take it as you leave home.

Best man's speech nerves

Some people would rather walk barefoot on hot coals than make a speech. Hopefully, the bridegroom, the bride's father, and the best man aren't among them. Having a quick drink is not a good solution; it may ease the pain of the speaker in the short term, but the audience is likely to suffer. Omega 3 is a good hedge against nerves, and should be taken for a week or so beforehand. The Ayurvedic remedy Brahmi Plus, which is often used for people taking exams, helps concentration. Again, Nelson's Rescue Remedy could be helpful if there's a sudden panic attack.

Overindulgence

It happens in the best of families. Someone mixes their drinks or quite simply drinks too much. You may even know in advance that someone is likely to overindulge. It's very hard to find a deterrent and worrying about it will take the edge off the day. If the likely culprit is a teenager, by all means try issuing dire warnings of social disgrace. Otherwise, you may have to let adults be adults and take their own consequences.

If someone does drink to excess, there are several good remedies that will help: have milk thistle to hand, or artichoke. There are also good brand-named products that you can pick up in advance from the chemist and keep in your emergencies kit.

Tip from Lindsay Gill of Healthspan:

If the bride spends all day on her feet and they start to hurt, rub a little vodka into them. This has the effect of numbing them. Apparently top models do this!

13 Flowers and favours

Flowers and weddings have always gone together. For centuries, brides and their attendants have carried flowers, which often held special meanings. For a time, white flowers for the bride were considered to symbolise purity, and roses and orange blossom have always been favoured because of their fragrance and associations of love.

Nowadays, flowers are often selected in colours to complement the bride's dress, and are used throughout the day to carry a theme from the wedding ceremony through to the reception. The choice of flowers is wider than it once was: from daffodils to sunflowers, from exotic blooms from the Cape of South Africa, to spring wild flowers and winter berries from English hedgerows.

Professional florists

The bigger florists will have a portfolio of bouquets and posies from which you can select a style and the blooms, according to season. Some will offer artificial and silk flowers too. Consulting the portfolios of several florists will give you a feel of price, and from this you can set a budget. Check for extras: wires, ribbons and trims, delivery and of course VAT.

If you don't have a recommendation, it may be worth checking that the florist has real experience of weddings. You will need to discuss how the flowers will be kept fresh on the day, particularly if it is an afternoon wedding, and how and where the transportation will be arranged. Don't forget to discuss how much will be required as a deposit.

Bridal flowers

There are four main styles of bridal flowers:

- a hand-tied posy that comprises short-stemmed flowers, tied with ribbons
- a more formal posy of tightly packed flowers, often rosebuds
- a bouquet of long-stemmed flowers, in a natural arrangement, tied loosely
- the traditional 'teardrop', a formal arrangement ending in a point.

Your height, the style of your wedding dress and the formality/informality of the wedding will all dictate which kind of arrangement of bridal flowers you choose. You may wish to take a drawing or photo of your dress, along with fabric samples, including trimmings, to your florist. You then must select the flowers that have meaning to you and which will be available at the time of your wedding. A good florist will also be able to help you with any flowers for a headdress.

It has long been a custom for the bride to toss her bouquet at the end of the celebrations, the tradition being that whichever young woman catches it will be the next to marry. Follow the practice by all means, but you can also make another gesture: present your flowers to the oldest lady present, or take them to someone who is housebound, or even put them on the grave of someone dear to you or to your new extended family.

Attendants' flowers

The bridesmaids' flowers usually echo – in a smaller form – those carried by the bride. There has been a fashion for having flowers in small baskets or in posy 'balls' or on hoops, but these only look appropriate for children or if there is a period feel to the dresses. Older bridesmaids would probably prefer a posy. Again, take drawings and fabric samples of the attendants' outfits to show the florist.

Flowers for the rest of the bridal party

Buttonholes for the bridegroom, best man, ushers, and fathers (or escorts), and corsages for the mothers of the bride and bridegroom usually contain at least some of the flowers – or reflect the colours – that the bride will carry in her bouquet or posy. It may be a good precaution to have a few extra buttonholes in case someone loses or forgets theirs during the run-up to the ceremony.

Flowers for the ceremony and reception

Flowers, flowers everywhere! If you are having a church wedding, you will need to speak to your minister about any restrictions on decorations within and around the church. Some brides elect to have flowers tied to the lych-gate and at the doorway as well as within the body of the church. Many venues have Guilds of Flower Arrangers. See Chapter 5 for further advice.

The registry office and their approved venues will all have provision for wedding flowers. Ask the registrar or the catering manager of a venue for guidance. Remember, they have done all this before!

If you wish, your flowers can be duplicated on any form of transport, and of course be a theme throughout your reception.

Wedding favours

There is still the charming tradition of bridal favours, small gifts to the wedding guests, usually placed on the tables at the reception. These can be floral, or tiny plants, or sweets. A whole industry has grown around producing tiny gift boxes and sachets. However, you can make these yourself, and this gives little presents real meaning. For example, you can tie sugared almonds or little cookies into a small piece of net with a pretty strip of ribbon.

The language of flowers

This was known by the Victorians as floriography and was used as a means of communication. Here are some flowers that carry a special message for brides:

Ambrosia – love returned
Aster – love, daintiness
Azalea – Chinese symbol of womanhood

Baby's Breath – everlasting love and happiness
Bells of Ireland – good luck

Carnation – bonds of affection
Carnation (white) – sweet and lovely, pure love
Chrysanthemum (red) – I love

Daisy – innocence, loyal love

Forget-me-not – true love

Gladiolus – love at first sight

Heather – good luck
Heliotrope – devotion, eternal love
Ivy – fidelity, marriage

Jonquil – love me, affection returned

Lilac – first love
Lily – purity

Lily of the valley – sweetness, return to happiness

Marjoram (sweet) – joy and happiness
Myrtle – love, Hebrew emblem of marriage

Orange blossom – purity, eternal love
Pansy – love
Peach blossom – I am your captive
Primrose – early love

Rose (red) – I love you
Rose (white) – eternal love
Rose (pink) – perfect happiness
Rose (red and white) – unity
Rosemary – remembrance, fidelity

Stephanotis – happiness in marriage
Veronica – fidelity
Zinnia (scarlet) – constancy

Courtesy of Chrissie Harten, www.thegardener.btinternet.co.uk

14 Rings, presents and other considerations

Rings

The majority of men as well as women now wear wedding rings, which traditionally are either made from gold or platinum. Recently there's been a fashion of having stones, usually diamond, set into the rings, both for men and women. Many jewellers now offer diamonds sourced from conflict-free areas of the world.

Brides will choose a ring to complement their engagement ring, and bridegrooms will often select one that echoes the style of their bride's. The size of the hands and length of fingers will probably influence the final choice too, so it's a good idea to try the rings on even if you know your ring size and have a recommended online supplier. Some couples will have an inscription engraved on the inner band, giving the wedding date, perhaps their initials and even a personal message.

Keep the receipts for insurance purposes.

Notices

You may wish to announce your engagement and wedding in the local, or even a national newspaper. The advertisement staff are usually adept at helping you with the wording, and you can 'book' the announcement well in advance.

Some local papers still carry wedding pictures. If yours does so, don't forget to brief your photographer accordingly or, if you will be honeymooning, arrange for your best man or chief bridesmaid to take the photograph and all the relevant details into the newspaper office as soon as possible after the wedding.

Wedding lists

There was a time when setting up a wedding list at a local department store was considered rather vulgar by some. Would-be present givers felt uncomfortable that the bride and bridegroom would know exactly how much they had spent – and somehow it looked as though you couldn't be bothered to find something a little more special.

How times have changed! Most couples now set up a wedding list in one form or another, knowing that family and friends, whether well-off or strapped, are short of time and would anyway like to make a gift that is both appropriate and required. With so many couples having a home – or homes – prior to their marriage, the 'bottom drawer' selection is likely to be very different from a young couple making a home from scratch.

Some couples who already have complete households now ask for 'vouchers' for a special honeymoon or towards a treat when on honeymoon, such as a balloon ride or a particular excursion. Others request donations to a favourite charity, or opt for a charity gift (see eco-presents on page 69).

Yet others decide they would like presents that upgrade their current possessions. For example, they may select more expensive tableware or beautiful linens. This fits exactly with the pattern of wedding present purchase. The givers usually wish to buy something that will last a lifetime, rather than masses of cheaper goods, however practical. Very few opt for electrical items.

Table and kitchenware, small furniture items – lamps, clocks, mirrors, pictures – and small heirlooms are still the choice of most couples, with garden and patio furniture and games equipment now featuring on some lists. Presents with a feelgood factor such as spiritual statues and Buddhas are also currently very popular.

Lists can be kept at a selected local department store, and some well-known national chains offer services. However, it is worth remembering that wedding lists are not these stores' main activity, and there is often limited choice from any one department and frequently little personal service or research. Often brides will want to know, for example, if a certain style of china is new and will still be available over a number of years. Store staff may not know this.

There is now more choice. Specialist wedding list shops have extensive showrooms and equally impressive websites, offering an immense range of products and suppliers from which lists can be made up. Usually the couple visits the showrooms, where there is a full consultation. Frequently this service is free of charge to the bride and groom. The advantages are that there is a wider selection of products available and a more personalised service, which may include sourcing particular items and obtaining expert advice.

Wedding list services recommend that couples set up their lists in advance of sending out their wedding invitations, and suggest keeping the list open for up to a year afterwards, covering the following Christmas or other major gift-giving celebrations such as birthdays.

Presents on the day

Most couples would prefer to have their presents before or after the wedding but not on the day itself. There is too much happening, too many people to meet and greet, and not enough time to show proper appreciation. It also means that someone has to look after the gifts, keep them in a safe place and transport them home afterwards.

Despite hints and outright requests on this matter, it's inevitable that one or two people – or even many more – will bring their presents anyway. Perhaps they live far away and their gift is fragile or, quite simply, they want to witness your delight.

Make sure that there will be somewhere appropriate and safe to leave presents at the reception or party venue. You may also wish to nominate a bridesmaid or an usher to have special responsibility for looking after the presents. As presents will be unwrapped by the bride and groom, they may lose their tags. And in all the excitement, you may forget precisely what is from whom. To avoid any embarrassment later, it may be a good idea for the bridesmaid or usher to keep a list – quietly and discreetly – of who gave what.

Thank yous

Many printers who specialise in wedding stationery offer a package that often includes 'save the date' cards, invitations, service sheets – and thank you postcards. All the bride and groom have to do afterwards is fill in the names of the givers and a swift description of the present. There you are, a chore done and dusted.

Of course, this is better than sending no thank you note at all, but some people – and the author is one of them – find this almost insulting. It is merely a form of receipt. When I have gone to the time and trouble of finding a gift that I truly hope will be liked if not loved, paying for it, wrapping it in gorgeous paper and ribbons, making sure it arrives safely, I would like a personal note by way of return. So you received hundreds of presents. Lucky you. Old-fashioned me, even if it is some weeks afterwards, I would still appreciate a proper individual THANK YOU!

Presents for attendants

It is traditional for the bride and bridegroom to give gifts to the best man, bridesmaids (and pageboys) and to the ushers as keepsakes of this special day. These usually take the form of jewellery for the bridesmaids, although an evening purse, photo frame or beautiful personal stationery might be equally acceptable. The best man's present could be a voucher for a special event, a decanter or tankard, wine glasses, pen or leather wallet. Ushers might welcome a special keyring, business card holder, book or calculator. Pageboys might prefer a sports bag, computer game or watch. A charming touch is to have their initials and perhaps a short message engraved or embossed on the present.

15 Capturing the event

Everyone hopes to have warm and happy recollections of their wedding that never fade. But, once the event is over – in one, five or ten years along life's path – the only accurate records will be the photographs and, if you so choose, the video. Sometimes it is tempting to economise, particularly if a friend or family member fancies themselves as an unsung Lord Snowdon. However, unless they are extremely gifted, it is unlikely that they can compete with the professionals.

This can leave some families in a dilemma: how to ensure that there is the highest quality photography without offending the dear friend or family member who is armed with their camera and the best intentions. One way round this may be to enlist the help of the would-be photographer to 'double up' on some shots to ensure that nothing is lost, or to assign them to photographs of a certain part of the day.

Finding the right photographer

It is well worth spending time on finding the right kind of photographer whose style suits you, and then briefing that photographer thoroughly. There are a number of avenues for you to try:

- Seek recommendations from friends who have been recently married or from wedding guests who have been impressed by the pictures.
- Look on the internet, particularly at those sites of professional organisations to which well qualified photographers will

belong. This implies that their work will be of a good standard. Organisations include the Society of Wedding and Portrait Photographers (www.swpp.co.uk), the Master Photographers Association (www.thempa.com), and the British Institute of Photographers (www.bipp.com).

Ask to see the portfolio of several photographers. You should very quickly be able to identify which one has the style and personality that you would like for your wedding. Obviously your budget will play an important part in your final choice; you need to establish exactly what the cost covers. One element you should consider is asking if the photographer uses Photoshop. This is a computer software package that enables the photographer to edit the photos, taking out minor flaws (the tree branch that appears to be growing out of the groom's ear, for example, or the shine on the bride's mother's forehead), adding modern artistic effects and 'cropping' the shots to enhance the atmosphere.

Julia Boggio, director of Julia Boggio Photography, always sees the bride and the bridegroom together, right from the outset. She explains: 'I am creating the first heirloom – the wedding album – for this new family unit. It's important that I understand the "story" of the day, so I can capture its essence. In order to do that, I like to establish a rapport and a level of trust. They don't want to be dealing with a stranger on their big day.'

The photography brief

Julia points out that her clients often ask for 'reportage' photographs. What they actually mean is natural-looking shots, as opposed to highly formal. In reality, obtaining that very natural shot often takes even more planning than the formal ones. With a photographer you like and get on well with, you can really enjoy creating these images.

Julia finds that to tell the story of the day effectively, she needs to use a variety of photographic styles, for example:

- documentary or reportage: for the 'natural' shots of the bride getting ready, of the bride with her attendants, with her escort (possibly her father, stepfather or brother), of the groom with his ushers, during the ceremony, and so on.
- traditional: to provide those group shots that parents like to have on their mantelpieces.
- fashion and glamour: for the photographs of the bride and groom on their special day.
- still life: the little details such as the shoes or a pile of bouquets and posies.
- the architecture and landscape: the venue and the surroundings of the wedding.

Responsible, professional photographers will also ask beforehand to speak to whoever is officiating at the wedding, that is, either the minister or the registrar. This is to establish where and when he or she will be welcome to take shots during the service, and when it would be considered intrusive.

Even when the photographer works with an assistant, a timed schedule is invaluable so that every aspect of the day can be covered. It is also important to have someone available to point out who is who, and to act as liaison for the photographer throughout the day. This is usually the best man, and it should be listed as part of his responsibilities. How else can the photographer know who should be rounded up for the big family shots? A photo list is essential, to make certain all the guests are included at appropriate points. Some photographers, like Julia, also offer to hold a post-honeymoon shoot. 'It's an emotional time – I cried non-stop throughout my own wedding day – so sometimes it is better to take portraits of the bride and groom at a later date when they are more relaxed.'

After the wedding, it is now common practice to put the pictures online, with a secured password, so family and friends can make their orders, and people from near and far, unable to attend, can see highlights of the day.

Cautionary tale: Patricia

Patricia has been married twice. The wedding of her son by her first marriage was attended by both her first husband with his new partner, and Patricia with her second husband. She explains that it had been a fairly acrimonious divorce, and neither were comfortable with one another or their new partners. Even so, over the years they had liaised on their son's education and they decided that it was only civilised to cope in each other's company for his wedding day.

The wedding went well but when it came to the wedding photographs, neither side wanted the picture for their mantelpieces showing their former partners. With a bit of negotiation, the set piece of bride and groom with their respective parents was taken twice, once with Patricia, her second husband and her son's new in-laws, the second with his father and partner and new in-laws.

Patricia's advice:

Brief the photographer in advance if there are sensitivities such as this, because he or she can then handle it in a very natural way and no one looks as though they are being awkward.

Videography

Choosing a suitable videographer requires much the same care and procedure as selecting your photographer. If you don't know of a videographer, you can:

- ask your chosen photographer, who will probably have worked with a number of videographers at other weddings and will know who is reliable and gifted
- ask other brides
- consult the professional organisations which, in this case, are: The Institute of Videography, which deals with professional standards

(www.iov.co.uk); the Association of Professional Videomakers (www.apv.org.uk) and the Wedding and Event Videographers Association, which offers lists internationally (www.weva.com). There is also a useful website: www.visualbride.co.uk which is an advertisement site but shows sample material.

Ask to see samples of the work of several videographers. As with photography, each one will have a distinctive style, and you should opt for the one whose work appeals to you most. It is also important that you trust your videographer. You should be able to talk to him or her easily and they in turn must be flexible. After all, this is your special day and the film should reflect it accurately.

Be sure that you know how the videographer plans to record sound – of speeches for example – and you should discuss the final format. It is well worth considering HD widescreen, since this is becoming standard for all new televisions.

You will probably be offered different inclusive 'packages', which will cover filming, editing and DVD production. The main differences between the packages will be whether they film some or all of the day, and what size crew they provide. For guidance, you will probably need only a one-man crew for a small or budget wedding of up to 80 guests. A two-man or more crew for a larger wedding means that the finished film will have more varied perspectives – guest's reactions and all the little details that make up the day – and enable filming of simultaneous events such as the bride's final preparations at the same time as people arriving at the ceremony. They may also allow the opportunity for guests to record their personal messages direct to the camera.

Be aware that the filming on the day is only a small part of the film-making process. The actual filming may only last one day (more for Asian weddings), but the editing will take up to four or five days. This is where the major part of the budget goes. Editing is the creative process that turns raw footage, which can often seem dull and monotonous, into a truly professional and fascinating film. It entails selecting the best material and arranging it in sequences that re-tell the story of the wedding in an entertaining and meaningful way.

Whichever videographer you choose, check that they have insurance and discuss the issue of copyright with them. Meet them before the wedding to plan it out properly. Some videographers would welcome visiting all the venues in advance and attending the rehearsal, for instance.

To guarantee the best results, Andrew Cussens, the creative director of Bloomsbury Films, a specialist wedding video company, advises that you help your videographer in the following ways:

- Build a schedule of the day.
- Confirm the name and contacts of whoever is officiating. Like the photographer, the videographer needs to know where and when filming is permissible, and when it would be inappropriate.
- List the special touches: the cousin who will be singing during the ceremony or the groom's plan to play in the band at the reception.
- Provide a list of the special guests – grandmothers and those coming long distances.
- Possibly provide small portrait photographs of the key players, because the videographer won't have the opportunity to be introduced on the day amidst all the excitement.
- Nominate the person with whom the videographer should liaise throughout the day. This again may be the best man.
- Give mobile phone numbers of the main party, not to be used during the proceedings but for early-morning checks.
- Suggest how you would like your photographer and videographers to be dressed. If it is a very formal wedding, say so and ask the filmmakers to be attired appropriately.

Andrew explains:

We aim to be discreet and unobtrusive, but at the same time we are making what will become a family documentary of 30 to 60 minutes – more if it is an Asian wedding. We need to know what is going on. No two wedding videos should ever be the same.

Ultimately a good film comes from the heart not the equipment. We're telling a story that involves everyone present. We aim to capture the magic for the couple themselves and the reactions of everyone around them. We don't just point and shoot, but reflect the essence of the day: the fragrance of the flowers, the weather and light, the little moments and intimacies between the guests. After all, you don't often have that number of family and friends together in one place!

After the editing comes the selection of music, which will seal the atmosphere of the film. Sometimes couples ask for favourite pieces, but it is worth listening to your videographer's suggestions for creating the right background and mood. Often they will provide not only the full DVD but also a shorter version of the highlights of the day. They may also put the highlights on to a special website in the couple's name, or upload it on to a site like YouTube so you can share it without lending your DVD.

16 Getting around

There's a lot of to-ing and fro-ing with a wedding. Usually, the bride and her party leave for the main ceremony from one address, the bridegroom and best man from another. Parents and other special guests may be coming from different directions. After the ceremony, the bridal party has to reach the reception venue. Photographs may hold things up, so other guests may preceed the bridal party.

There is an enormous range of options for the transportation for the bridal party and the bridegroom to reach the ceremony, most usually:

- family cars
- chauffeur-driven cars or limousines
- a hired sports car for the bridegroom and best man
- taxis.

For the post-service transport for the bride and groom, you could consider:

- family cars, chauffeur driven cars or taxis
- a vintage motor car
- horse-drawn carriages
- a milk float or golf cart (suitably decorated, of course!)
- a rickshaw.

For the main party:

- London Routemaster bus

- coach
- minibus.

Remember that if the bridal dress is long, and there's perhaps a veil as well, you will require more room. You may well be squashed and therefore in danger of creasing your dress in a modern car. Vintage cars and taxis allow much more space. The chauffeur of a limousine will also know how to arrange your dress so that when you alight, it will flow out behind you.

Whatever the choice, brides may wish to consider the *colour* of the vehicle in which they travel. Paul Mackley of Perfect Day Cars and No-Prob-Limo in Leicestershire explains that if a bride is wearing white and she is photographed against a white car, her dress will blend in or even 'disappear'. A white car will not do justice to dresses in subtle colours such as champagne, cream, oyster or ivory. They will tend to look lacklustre against the hard whiteness of car paintwork. Choose a burgundy, blue or two-tone car instead.

He recommends that when booking wedding cars, you also consider the following:

- Ensure that your car and driver are booked out to you for the day so that if there's a hold-up – maybe your photos are taking longer than anticipated – your car is still available and the driver waiting happily, not rushing off to another wedding. This can work both ways. If the wedding car company has other weddings on the same day and is using the same cars, delays in someone else's wedding could hold up your arrangements.
- Check that the wedding car company has an alternative vehicle. As Paul points out, even the most prestigious cars can occasionally develop problems.
- You can choose one car to make several trips to transport not only the bride and her escort and bridesmaids but also the mothers of the bride and bridegroom. Alternatively you can

book two or more cars to arrive in procession, which will create more impact.

- Always allow plenty of time for the journey to the church or wedding venue. Ask the wedding car company to check if there are roadworks, a busy shopping street or a major event such as a football match on your routes.

- Don't forget to take fabric samples with you. Wedding car companies often have a selection of coloured ribbons to decorate the cars and, unless you are providing them yourself, they will try to match up the flowers for the car bonnet too. And some, like Perfect Day Cars, will have champagne or non-alcoholic champagne waiting for the bride and groom after the service!

17 Wedding receptions: venues and food

Venues

Professional planners will tell you that they spend about a quarter of their time organising the venue for the reception. As mentioned before, the accepted wisdom is that it should be only twenty minutes from wherever the service has been held. This way people don't get lost, stuck in traffic from local events, overheated and irritable.

Finding the perfect venue is an art form. It's not just a question of finding a pretty spot. The elements to consider are:

- the right size for your number of guests
- the kind of facilities you require – changing facilities for the bride and groom, perhaps a crèche for babies and small children, backdrops for photographs
- kitchen facilities for outside (or your own) catering
- car parking and access for wheelchairs
- the shape of the dining space if you are having a meal, the acoustics for speeches, room for dancing
- the quality of catering, both food and wines, if only in-house catering is permitted
- an acceptable price.

Nowadays, all kinds of venues are on offer for wedding parties, and each of these have advantages and drawbacks, but first look at the range:

- National treasures: such as the Science Museum, the Design Museum and Blenheim Palace, along with certain National Trust and English Heritage properties. These unique properties can sometimes be hired for the wedding service – where the property is an approved premises – as well as the function that follows.
- Approved premises: as mentioned previously, each registry office will have a range of approved premises within their locality, and these may include town halls, orangeries, galleries and hotels.
- Restaurants: for reception parties only
- Hotels: where these are not on the approved premises list, they would be for reception parties only. Look in glossy travel magazines and county magazines for adverts and reviews of new hotels.
- Village halls or club rooms
- A marquee: in your garden if it is big enough, or with permission on private ground elsewhere such as a farmer's field.
- The unusual: a vineyard, a yacht, roof garden.

Check points

Each of these require a different approach, although there are some points to check that are common to all:

- Check what time the bar closes. You may require a licence extension in some venues.
- Confirm that there is public liability insurance.
- Know your contractual obligations. For instance, there may be a minimum number. Check if you would be eligible for payment if there are fewer people on the day.
- Investigate any limitations relating to noise levels, use of candles and fireworks, and security.
- Look for hidden costs such as flowers, service charges and VAT.

- Be sure there is enough car parking for the likely number of guests.
- Look at the facilities for changing – including baby changing – if you or your guests are likely to require them.
- Check disabled access.

National treasures

These may be very beautiful but they may impose certain restrictions. Check:

- Exclusivity. You don't want to find that there are several wedding parties at the same venue, albeit in different catering suites, all queuing for photography around the fountain. Check what else is happening during the period you wish to be there.
- Access. You may not be able to gain access during the hours that the general public are in the building.
- Candles. Naked lights, such as candles, may be prohibited.
- Sound. There may be house rules relating to sound levels, and any sound at all after a certain time.
- Objet d'Art. You may not be able to move paintings or pieces of furniture or install extra lighting (for photography) without prior consent, and in some instances, there may even be a charge for the appropriately insured people to move the objects.
- Insurance. Where a building is very old and fragile, or there are precious items and hangings in situ, be sure to know that you are covered if a member of your party causes any damage.
- Ancillary costs. These may include security staff.
- Hotels. If you do not live nearby, the bridal party, as well as guests travelling long distances, will require accommodation. Check to see that there are hotels of the right quality nearby.

Approved premises

Remember that the registrar will only attend to take the service between 8 a.m. and 6 p.m., which means that the latest wedding can be scheduled is 5 p.m.

Restaurants

Consider whether you want an exclusive space, perhaps for a smaller party or, for a larger event, the restaurant to be exclusively yours. Be aware that few restaurants will want to be closed to ordinary diners on popular evenings such as Saturdays, but they may offer exclusivity on other nights in the week or lunchtimes.

Hotels

Different kinds of hotels have different patterns of business. Special hotels – those in the country or in venues that attract weekenders – will probably have more availability midweek. Alternatively, hotels that attract businesspeople during the week may well have more availability at weekends. They may even offer preferential rates at less busy times.

If you have a number of guests staying at the hotel, it is also worth trying to negotiate a room upgrade for the bridal party.

If you choose to hold the service and/or reception at a hotel, it is also worth establishing a dedicated contact within the hotel's banqueting or hospitality team.

Village halls or club rooms

The main thing is to be very clear about what can be provided within the hall and club, and what has to be brought in by way of catering equipment and such things as tableware, cutlery, ice for wine buckets – the *corkscrew* – glasses, extra furniture and so on. If you are arranging the catering or doing it yourself, it would be wise to be certain that there are enough helpers on hand.

Ensure that there is adequate space for coats, umbrellas and baby buggies, and somewhere safe to leave presents if people are likely to bring them.

You may wish to decorate the room. Swathes of fabric, large plants, huge bunches of balloons and banners can all help hide immovable items that you find unattractive. Check when you can have access to lay out the room as you wish and to bring in all the items you require, and that there is a cool place to leave dry foodstuffs and flowers, and fridge space for wines and items that need to be kept chilled.

If necessary arrange for someone to come in and look after deliveries on the day – the flowers and wedding cake for example – with a list of phone numbers so contact can be made if these precious items fail to show up on time.

It may be appropriate to ask if you can have reserved parking spaces for the bridal party's cars – for the bride and bridegroom certainly, and maybe also the bridesmaids, best man and ushers, and the parents – ensuring that the spaces are near to the door.

Marquees

Research and select a reputable marquee company and they will help you choose the kind of structure – an original tent form or a rigid free-standing metal frame tent – the lining, flooring, pathway, furniture (tables and chairs), platforms, PA system, lighting inside and out, generator, access to lavatories (or to the house). Then work with the company on the mechanism – and access – for setting up the marquee and dismantling it after the function.

Always ask for a detailed quotation, showing insurance cover and VAT, and ensure that you accept it in writing.

Be aware that you now have to find caterers and florists who can work around the time of the marquee being properly assembled and dismantled.

Other venues

If you are feeling adventurous, you may be looking for an unusual venue that is rarely available. Good for you. Just be aware that, if it is outdoors, it is well worth having a poor weather programme. If the rain has lashed down for 24 hours beforehand, your vineyard, for instance, may be a sea of mud. Wellington boots and a wedding dress would be memorable, but your guests need to be prepared. And if it is still lashing with rain, you will need a dry alternative!

Also consider what might happen if someone had an accident or had lost or damaged property. Would they sue you? Check with a good insurance agent because, like the rain forecast, it is better to be safe than sorry.

Otherwise, the requirements are much the same as if you were having your event in a hall or club.

Themes

Nowadays, many people choose a theme for their reception: Indian, reggae, *Great Gatsby* or circus, and this gives scope for decoration and entertainment. It may be worth remembering that many weddings are major family gatherings. If you are having a wedding that is mainly for your friends, that is, predominantly for one age group, a theme may be a perfect way to give the reception a lift and make it different from other parties. However, if it is a gathering of the clans, with lots of different age groups, it may be wise to ensure that your theme is one that everyone will enjoy and appreciate, not just your buddies.

Food

Catering

As with so many aspects of wedding celebrations, the traditional sit-down meal of four or more courses is no longer obligatory. You can still opt for the formal starter-fish-meat-sweets-cheeses kind of banquet but, for all except the grandest weddings, a lighter, more creative menu is usually more appropriate. Palates in the UK have become more sophisticated as we are exposed to a wider variety of foods from all over the world, both in our supermarkets and in restaurants. People are more food-aware and diet-conscious too. Allow for a number of vegetarians. If you are not sure how many, your caterer will probably suggest at least a quarter of the food is suitable. If you are having local or organic produce for a proportion of the dishes, find a way to let people know, either on the menu cards or, if it is a buffet, on little 'tent' cards.

If you are having a theme to your reception party, you may wish to reflect this in the food. Do remember that children and much older people can be quite conservative in their tastes so, if you are having, for instance, Moroccan food, be sure there is something recognisably plainer available.

Self-catering

If it is a very intimate wedding and you enjoy cooking or you are a caterer by profession, then by all means arrange the catering yourself. If not, with all the other aspects of your wedding that will demand attention, it may be prudent to find willing family and friends to take responsibility. A light brunch, buffet or tea meal are the easiest to cater for, both in terms of preparation, equipment on site, and freshness.

There's a lot to be said for paper tablecloths and napkins and very basic china and cutlery. You can always cheer up the tables with candles, balloons, flowers and favours.

If you decide that you wish for a sit-down meal, ensure that there is sufficient of everything: cutlery, china, glasses, cruets, finger bowls or whatever. Consider hiring waitresses or finding truly responsible young people.

Buffets come in two forms. The finger buffet consists of bite-sized pieces that may warrant a plate but don't require cutlery. Allow at least fifteen items per person. It is recommended that some chairs and tables are provided. While the majority of guests may be happy to stand juggling their plates and glasses, the very old and the pregnant may be all too delighted to sit down.

The fork buffet is usually a full spread of cold meats, pasta, salads and maybe some hot dishes as well. Tables and cutlery will therefore be required. If you have a lot of guests, it may be worth having two or more smaller serving tables, rather than one long larger one. Puddings and desserts can be served from different points, or at a later time from the same tables.

Cake

It used to be a many-tiered, heavily fruited affair, with marzipan and hard white icing. It was never to everyone's taste! Now you can have a luscious chocolate cake, lemon cake or carrot cake, a concoction of sugared roses, a raft of meringues or a column of crystallised fruit.

Your wedding reception venue may be able to offer a superb cake-making service. Alternatively you may prefer to arrange your own cake. If you don't have a recommendation, or an inspired and talented cook within your circle, check your best local bakeries, and some of the specialist wedding cake-makers that offer a national service. Be aware that the cost of the more elaborate creations is quite high.

Be sure to check and double-check what kind of cake stand you will require, and what kind of knife you will need to cut it.

Drinks

No wedding would be quite complete without a glass of bubbles, certainly for the toasts. Champagne means French champagne, but there are some wonderful sparkling wines from other countries, made by the same method, that taste every bit as delicious but don't cost quite so much. Be sure to have a non-alcoholic bubbly drink, such as sparkling apple or elderflower, available for children and non-drinkers.

To greet the reception guests, you can certainly offer sparkling wine, but it may be fun to offer cocktails decorated with pretty fruits and edible flowers, or Pimms. Create a special cocktail yourself – or give this task to the bridegroom – and give it an appropriate name.

Not everyone likes wine, so be sure there are some beers and soft drinks available too.

Self-catering

If you are self-catering, source your drinks from a supplier who will do 'sale or return'. Some will offer a loan service for glasses. Be aware that some venues will charge corkage if you bring your own drinks. Corkage is a set amount charged on every bottle opened, whether champagne or fruit juice.

It has always been customary to serve red wines with red meats and dry white wines with white meat – that is, chicken and fish. Sweet white wines complement puddings and desserts. Except for the most formal dinners, people don't tend to stick to these guidelines anymore, but simply drink what they enjoy. However, red wine should never be served before white because it tends to overpower the palate.

Champagnes, sparkling wine and still white wines benefit from being served slightly chilled. If too cold, champagne and sparkling wines will froth all over the glasses and so take an age to serve. Be careful about putting sparkling wine into a freezer as, if left for too long, the bottles will burst. Stick to the fridge or an ice-bucket.

Allow about half a bottle of wine per guest, adjusting the amount downwards if a lot of people will be driving after the meal. Have plenty of soft drinks available for drivers – and other people will want them if you have a lot of dancing.

Don't forget to have several corkscrews and bottle openers.

For the children

If you have small children attending the reception, make their day special by providing them with some form of entertainment fairly early on. Depending on the style of the reception, you can even create a play-table with games, activity books and crayons. If it is likely to be a large group of children, you may decide to have a separate room and a 'minder'. Other celebratory distractions might be those little bottles of bubbles that children can blow about with safety, or you can give them all a disposable camera. Then they can really join in the fun!

Cautionary tale: Pat

Pat's son is marrying a girl who is organising the wedding with her mother. Her problem is that the bride has decided she does not want children at the wedding breakfast. Pat's relatives are coming over from France and they have several small children that they won't want to leave behind. She realised there will be other people in the same quandary.

Pat's solution:

We have offered to arrange for a crèche in a hotel nearby. We are organising for a team of qualified babysitters to hold a little party especially for them, with hats and games and a cake. We might even ask the bride to pop in and visit them. They will adore that.

18 Wedding receptions: form and style

Seating plans

A wedding is a major gathering of the clans when sometimes people haven't seen each other for many years. Old allegiances and, sadly, old rivalries are likely to surface. At the same time, members of the bride's family will probably not know members of the bridegroom's family. The whole idea is to bring the two families together. However, in the process sometimes dear friends are pushed aside, amid all the family hierarchy. This makes the seating plan for a sit-down wedding breakfast all the more important. In some families, it will require the skills of highest diplomacy!

Even if yours is the most congenial of gatherings you should have a plan for the top table. The bride and bridegroom take central place, of course, and then it is up to you whether you seat the bride's and bridegroom's parents together with their respective partners, or split them up so they sit with the other's partner.

The classic pattern is, left to right: chief bridesmaid, bridegroom's father, bride's mother, bridegroom, bride, bride's father, bridegroom's mother, best man. Step-parents can be seated at the far ends of the table, and if both sets of parents have remarried and they don't mix comfortably, you may wish to have a much longer table, and invite other attendants to dilute the group.

Where there are awkward family groupings, you could choose to have a circular top table, rather than a long one facing the 'body' of the room. You can have individual circular tables throughout if it pleases you and is more appropriate, rather than the old-fashioned format of a long table with extensions at right angles. This can sometimes be helpful when the hierarchy of the family is complicated.

Once the top table plan is established, it is up to you whether you allow people to sit where they will – which for small weddings where everyone is good friends is entirely suitable – or whether you devise a plan.

Certainly a seating plan for bigger weddings is a better bet. People seat themselves much quicker and you won't have any single chair gaps. Your knowledge of your guests and their relationships should help to iron out any awkwardness, and at the same time absorb anyone who doesn't know any of the other guests. Single guests will be delighted if they are seated with a lively mixed group, or put with one or two other single guests who will soon strike up conversations. Use one large easel to show the plans for a small wedding, several for a bigger wedding.

One charming custom that prevails in parts of Scandinavia is to have a list on each dining chair of all the guests, with one sentence about each of them. For instance: 'Maudy Graham, aunt of the bride, made the cake'; 'Andrew McIntosh, fellow student of the groom at Stirling University' or 'Mrs Flora Wright: long-time neighbour of the bride's family'. Use a highlighter to pick out those sitting at each table. The result is that everyone has a starting point for a conversation, and the event will be all the livelier for it.

Toastmasters

Despite their name, good toastmasters are really complete masters of ceremony. They will organise the seamless running of a reception from even before the time of arrival at the venue to the end of the proceedings, with the aim of permitting the bride and bridegroom – and their families – to concentrate on enjoying their special day.

Some venues will offer the services of a master of ceremony but it is worth ensuring that he or she is properly trained and preferably a member of one of the recognised organisations such as the National

Association of Toastmasters. Check their website directory both for general helpful information and for a directory of members (www.natuk.com).

Formal weddings, be they for 40 or 4,000, can benefit from this kind of elegant event organisation. Usually the toastmaster will arrange to see the bride or wedding organiser several months in advance to work out the style and, most importantly, the timings of the event. This will start with the likely duration of the service, the estimated time of travel to the reception venue, a short period for everyone to spruce up, and then the reception procedure itself. The discussion will also cover practical details, such as the wet and dry arrangements if there is a marquee. Your toastmaster will be able to help you with the logical drawing up of a seating plan, and the correct seating of the top table. You will need to be able to talk frankly to him or her, particularly if there are any family sensitivities to be taken into account.

A professional toastmaster will check every detail at the venue before guests arrive: the placing of name cards on the top table, the sound levels and batteries for microphones, the knife for the cutting of the cake and so on, liaising with the caterers or banquet manager. He or she will also assist the photographer by having a list of 'set' groups, and calling up guests to take part as required.

Among the decisions to be made for the reception is whether there will be a receiving line, and who will be in the receiving line party. When in doubt, simply opt for the bride and bridegroom. All of this will affect the timings, and therefore the chef and his staff. The rule of thumb is to allow half an hour per 100 guests. The toastmaster will then organise the receiving line on the day, announcing each guest to the bridal party before finally escorting the bride and groom to the top table. Your toastmaster will ask you if you wish grace to be said before the meal, and establish who will say it. If you are having a religious service and the minister is present, he or she would be the obvious choice. Otherwise the bride's father or another family member might wish to undertake this role, or the toastmaster will step in.

There will also have to be a decision about when the speeches should be held. Increasingly speeches are held before the meal and this again has implications for the chef and his team, and for when the caterer should serve the champagne for the toasts.

An experienced toastmaster will be able to support those who are making speeches, suggesting content and length, and helping with any last-minute nerves. After the speeches he or she will arrange and announce the cutting of the cake.

Finally, the toastmaster will close the formalities and announce the following entertainment, perhaps inviting the bride and her groom to lead off the dancing.

Peter Craft, secretary of the National Association of Toastmasters, says:

The smooth running of the day is down to the detailed preparation beforehand. Timing is all. You should have complete confidence in your choice of toastmaster, trust him or her and feel comfortable with their personality. Look for flexibility. It's up to the bride and bridegroom if they want to move away from tradition. After all, it's not our day but theirs.

Speeches

At some weddings, the speeches are held before the meal, largely to allow the speakers to enjoy the rest of the reception or party. It is well known that the vast majority of people would rather have their teeth extracted without anaesthetic than stand up and speak in public. Few can do so easily unless they have either had training or a lifetime's experience. However, even teachers and actors have been known to quail when they have to both write the script and deliver it before people they know and love in the middle of such a special event.

Traditionally – and there's no reason why you cannot break with this tradition if you so wish – there are three speeches, usually announced by the toastmaster or best man:

- The father of the bride – or whoever escorted her to the wedding ceremony – who welcomes everyone and thanks them for coming. He may then talk about the bride and how she met the bridegroom. He then asks for a toast to the newly married couple.

- The bridegroom – who speaks on behalf of the bride as well as himself, thanking the previous speaker, and also the respective parents. He compliments the bride and may speak about their wishes for the future. He finishes by thanking his best man, the bridesmaids, pageboys and any others who have contributed towards the day. He then proposes a toast to the bridesmaids (and pageboys).

- The best man – thanks the bridegroom for his toast and offers his congratulations to the bride and groom. He may then tell a few amusing stories about the groom's childhood. He may propose a toast to absent friends and read out any special greetings cards and messages. He may then announce the cutting of the cake.

Whole books, including two in this series – *Perfect Best Man* and *Perfect Wedding Speeches and Toasts* – and an increasing number of websites are dedicated to best man, bridegroom and father of the bride speeches. One new company, Oh Crikey! is expanding rapidly through offering short training courses in venues all over the country for fathers, bridegrooms and best men. It's such a good idea!

The received wisdom is as follows:

Content

- Keep it to a reasonable length. About seven or eight minutes is the longest you should aim for.

- Time yourself at a normal reading speed, then add two or three minutes to allow for whoops, cheers and other applause. When in doubt, keep it shorter rather than longer. People who drone on and on tend to send their audience to sleep. A long speech requires a consummate performer.

- Draft it out well in advance. Don't wait for last-minute inspiration: it may not come. By preparing in advance, you can hone and polish it, and add witticisms that suddenly occur to you. You can also try it out on a well trusted chum.

- Don't feel you have to be a professional scriptwriter. They are a special breed with a very rare gift. Aim for lightness and charm. Avoid any attempt at cleverness or anything remotely risqué. This is a day to remember for its magic, not for its embarrassing moments.
- Remember you have all generations in your audience, old and young, and if it is a multicultural wedding, people from different backgrounds who may have different ideas of what is acceptable as amusing. Best to play safe.
- Flatter, compliment and thank everyone. The bridegroom's responsibility is to thank the bridesmaids and the ushers. Fathers of the bride should thank their wives and families, the minister, the groom's family and anyone else who requires special mention, such as the very elderly or those who have travelled long distances.
- Don't be critical of anyone or of the venue or food. These have been carefully chosen and, even if the motif on the chicken was upside down, don't make a feature of it. It's best forgotten.
- Best men should avoid double entendres, and any mention of former partners of either of the couple. They can of course recount genuinely funny or amusing anecdotes about the bridegroom, his childhood and teenage years, his sports, hobbies or talents. Go carefully on personal habits, however.

Performance

- The trick is to stand firmly, with your weight spread evenly on both feet. Feel grounded. With shoulders back and chest open, breathe deeply before starting. Nerves often make people breathe through the top of their lungs, with the result that their first words come out as a squeak. Actors will tell you to calm your heartbeat by taking a deep breath, filling the bottom of your lungs, and letting it out smoothly and slowly.

- Use notes rather than a full word-by-word script, which doesn't usually work when said out loud anyway. It becomes stilted and, well, wordy!

- Practise, practise and practise, and then rehearse it again. All the best actors and entertainers do this in order to perfect their timing. Be yourself, look briefly at everyone individually, no staring, no looking vaguely over everyone's heads. Aim for natural.

- No one is expecting Billy Connolly, Rory Bremner or Lenny Henry, and remember, your guests are all ready to enjoy themselves, to laugh and have a good time. So ease up. Enjoy it yourself.

Leading off the dance

Often afternoon weddings end with a dance rather than a sit-down meal. Whatever the style of your dance – disco, traditional or a mixture – it is usual for the bride and bridegroom to lead off for the first dance, to be joined by the respective parents and the best man and chief bridesmaid. This can be a trial for one or both of the bridal couple, if dancing is something they normally avoid. Rather than make this a point of dread in the day, why not tackle the problem head-on and take your two – or four – left feet for a few dance lessons? Many dance teachers would be pleased to help you. Some dance teachers will even come along to your reception and instruct all the guests in a certain dance, as part of the general entertainment!

One couple, Julia Boggio and her husband, James, made a feature of their lead-off dance by performing a version of the famous dance from the film 'Dirty Dancing'. They posted film of their dance on the website YouTube and found themselves minor celebrities for a time.

However you arrange your dance, remember again that different generations enjoy different kinds of music, and that some people at your wedding may be single, divorced or widowed but still enjoy dancing. Have at least a few dances where everyone, old and young, can get up and join in the fun together. This is what good memories for all your guests are made from.

Other entertainments

The limit is only that of your imagination. You can opt for any kind of entertainment:

- jugglers and acrobats
- a string quartet playing Bach or Schubert
- a harpist
- shanty singers
- a jazz band
- a concert pianist
- mime artists
- a 60s rock and roll band
- bouncy castle
- old time music hall singsong
- an opera soloist
- a mobile casino
- a stand-up comedian.

There are so many more . . .

If you are hiring a good old-fashioned disco with a DJ, be sure to see the DJ in action on a previous occasion. A DJ can kill an event by playing the wrong kind of music or adopting a tone that is inappropriate. If you don't want any jokes or references to the bride and bridegroom's wedding night, brief him accordingly. A good DJ will act as a master of ceremonies for the party and will plan the music and elements of his script with you. You should also check that he has both public liability insurance and a portable appliance test certificate to cover his kit.

There is a National Association of Disc Jockeys, members of whom have all the requisite insurance and a code of practice. See www.ukdisco.co.uk and www.nadj.org.uk.

Quick reference 1: The master checklist

Of course, every wedding will be different and so the master checklist for your wedding will be particular to you. Use the following as a guide to make up your own 'to do' list. You can change its shape to make it work for you. You may wish to have it in time order, what to do when, or as we have it here, task by task. Add in every element, no matter how small. The smooth running of all major events comes down to the detail.

It can be quite useful to put the initials of the person undertaking each task alongside the listing. Where appropriate, add in the date by which the task must be completed. Give everyone a copy of the list. That way, no one can turn around and announce that they didn't realise they were supposed to be doing such-and-such.

Decision-making

- what kind of ceremony: civil or religious
- home or abroad
- who the main organiser will be
- what level of budget
- the ideal dates.

Next steps

- Decide who you would like to form the bridal party and check they are willing and available. Bring the team together and ensure that they know what their roles entail.
- Consider sending 'save the date' cards.
- Consider the style: informal, formal, budget, green.
- Check if hotel reservations will be needed for special guests to stay.
- Check validity of passports.
- Consider purchasing wedding insurance.

A religious service

- See the minister, priest or pastor.
- Confirm the date.
- Decide what extras you would like: the verger, bells, organist, choir, flowers.
- Discuss the form of service including readings and hymns.
- Confirm who will be printing the service sheet.
- Set a date for the rehearsal.
- Ensure that the full bridal party is available for the rehearsal.
- Check the form for car parking, wheelchair access, the policy on confetti, and on photography and videography during the service.

Civil

- Arrange an appointment with the local registry office.
- Collect together all necessary documentation.
- Decide room size/consider approved venues.
- If you wish for a humanist wedding, locate your nearest minister and make an appointment.

- Decide extras: toastmaster (as master of ceremonies), music, hymns and readings.
- Check with the registrar that your readings and hymn choices are acceptable.
- Decide flowers and other decoration and the policy on confetti.

Weddings abroad

- Consider if you wish for a civil service in the UK followed by a service of blessing abroad, or whether you wish for a foreign wedding service.
- Consider options offered by travel companies and specialist overseas wedding planners.
- Contact the London-based embassy, consulate or high commission of the country you wish to be married in. They will offer guidance on the procedure, the legal documentation required, the pre-wedding residency requirement and any visas or medical necessities.
- Make arrangements for any translation of your official documents.
- Consider the need for a translator in the country of your choice.
- Confirm that the passports of all your party are valid for the trip.
- Arrange any vaccinations and take a first-aid kit.

Pre-wedding celebrations

- Decide if you will have a joint pre-wedding party with your partner or separate celebrations.
- Consider your options for a honeymoon and make bookings.

Ensure that passports are current if you are holidaying abroad, and decide if the bride wishes to update her passport in her married name.

Dressing up

- Decide style – formal or informal – and consider colours, fabric and themes.
- Choose the bride's dress.
- If possible obtain samples of fabric and samples of trims.
- Choose appropriate underwear.
- Choose attendants' outfits.
- If necessary, arrange a schedule of fittings.
- Choose accessories including shoes.
- Decide bridegroom's outfit.
- Decide on hair and make-up for bride and attendants and make all appointments well in advance.
- Make an emergency kit for any necessary running repairs during the day.
- Take care of yourself. Check the health options.

Flowers and favours

- Decide if you will use a professional florist.
- If so, see portfolios.
- Set the budget; check on any extras.
- Select designs and flowers for: the bride, attendants, button-holes, service venue, reception venue and hire car. Take fabric and trim samples to match up the ribbons for flowers.
- Arrange storage and the various deliveries.
- Pay deposit.
- Consider if you wish to give wedding favours at the reception,

and if so, what kind. If they are floral, add to the list for your florist.

- Source your favours (or make them yourself) and ensure they are on the list for delivery to your reception venue.

Rings, presents & other things

- Make a date for the bride and bridegroom to select their wedding rings.
- Decide if the rings will be engraved.
- Ensure that the rings are collected and delivered to the best man for safekeeping.
- Keep the receipt for insurance purposes.
- If you wish to announce your wedding, book the notice in advance with the newspaper of your choice.
- Decide if you will open a wedding list and choose a department store, shop chain or wedding list service.
- Make an appointment to select items for your list.
- Arrange for wedding presents to be kept safely if given on the day. Ask a bridesmaid or usher to keep a list of who gave what.
- Make a list of the thank-you notes you will make after the wedding.
- Select presents for the bridal party, traditionally, gifts for the best man, bridesmaids, pageboys and ushers.

Photography and videography

- Decide if you wish to have professional photography and videography.
- See portfolios of photographers/videographers.
- Arrange a meeting to discuss requirements and style.
- Put together a list of special guests and special requirements.

- If you are having a religious service, put the photographer/ videographer in touch with the minister.
- Brief your best man or an usher to look after the photographer and point out people in the bridal party and special guests.

Invitations

- Collate your guest list.
- Decide if they will be formal or informal or a personal letter or note.
- Draft wording and select stationer.
- Decide what other information guests require, including directions for travel.
- Decide if you wish to enclose a reply card.

Transport

- Make a plan for how the bridal party – bride, escort, attendants, and parents of the couple, will arrive at the venue of the ceremony. Consider how the bridegroom and best man will arrive for the ceremony. Look at how the wedding party will then attend the reception.
- Make your travel plans accordingly.
- If you are booking vehicles, ensure that you have exclusive rights on the day.
- Allow plenty of time in your schedule for traffic and other hold-ups.

The reception: venues and food

- Make a list of your requirements: guest numbers, changing facilities, quality of catering, car parking and so on.

- Make a sweep of the venues that appeal to you. See catering and banqueting managers and see what they can provide for your budget.
- Decide menus, including a number of vegetarian dishes and meals for children, and select wines.
- Check exclusivity, and any restrictions relating to noise and the serving of alcohol.
- Make a booking in writing, with all details spelled out.
- If necessary, ask for maps and local transport arrangements that you can send on to your guests.
- Confirm room layout, a PA system for speeches, flowers and decoration and access times.
- Confirm final numbers two days before the event.
- Confirm facilities for any entertainers, bands or disco equipment.
- Consider having a play area for small children, or a crèche or separate party for them.
- If you are self-catering, check what equipment is available on site, when you can have access to the premises on the day, whether you can decorate the space, and check about public liability insurance and any health and safety issues.
- Check availability of fridge space for both food and wines.
- Consider asking for help from others, both for food and serving it, and create a menu that is manageable.
- Find a drinks supplier, see if sale or return is possible, and check hire of glasses. Don't forget to have several corkscrews.
- Arrange decorations and flowers.
- If you are having a marquee, consider time required for assembly and dismantling, since this will affect the schedule of florists and caterers.
- Outdoor venues: have a wet weather alternative! Check about access and public liability insurance.
- Choose your wedding cake or find someone who will make it for you. Arrange delivery and, if self-catering, ensure that there is a suitable knife available to cut it with.

Reception: form & style

- Decide the seating plan, according to the scale and formality of your reception. Request easels if it is a large event.
- Decide if you wish to engage a professional toastmaster. If so, arrange a briefing meeting.
- Decide what speeches you want to have. Encourage the speakers to practise. See if microphones are required.
- If you are having a dance afterwards, consider a few dance classes if you are going to lead off.
- Try to see performances by any entertainer or disc jockey you are considering. Book them by letter, confirming their fee and the duration of their performance. Ensure any necessary insurance is in place.

And finally

There's an old trick that professional event organisers sometimes use to make sure that all the details are in place. Pretend that you are a guest at your wedding. Imagine travelling to the venue of the ceremony, how you will park, how you are greeted and shown to your seat, what happens during the service, what happens afterwards, how you will go on to the reception, where you will put your coat or an umbrella, and so on . . .

Play the same game, but for each of the key members of the bridal party. This will remind you of what items to be delivered to each venue, who requires facilities and special support (the photographer, for example) and what needs special attention.

Make lists, work at it, then let it go. It's a wedding, CELEBRATE!

Quick reference 2: The legal part

Both bride and bridegroom must be 18 years old or above. If either party is under 18 but over 16 years old, parents or legal guardians will be required to give their formal consent in writing. No one under 16 can be married. The same age requirements – and consent – also apply to those entering civil partnerships.

The bride and groom or civil partners will also have to prove their ages, marital status, address and nationality. This usually means showing a birth certificate, current passport, identity card or Home Office Travel Document to the minister or registrar.

If either party has been married or in a civil partnership previously, they will need to show a Decree Absolute of Divorce or a Civil Partnership Dissolution. If a previous partner has died, then their death certificate, along with the original marriage certificate, will be required.

If the wedding is to take place abroad, the couple should seek advice from the embassy of the relevant country in order to establish what documentation is required by the host registrar or celebrant.

Pre-marital or pre-nuptial agreements

There is a new as yet relatively minor trend in the UK towards making a pre-marriage agreement between the bride and bridegroom – or civil partners – about how their assets would be split in the event of their marriage failing.

These have been common in other parts of the world, notably the USA and South Africa, and may be deemed practical – if a little negative

– in this country, where one partner is bringing significantly more wealth to the marriage than the other. However, at the time of writing, pre-marital contracts do not have any legal standing, and a divorce court can discount the agreement when making a settlement if it deems it unfair to one partner, or where there are children involved.

However, it is possible that future governments will look favourably on this trend, particularly for instances when there are only two people involved and property can be divided relatively easily without expensive court proceedings.

Wills

Under British law, when a husband or wife dies without any children the surviving spouse automatically inherits the entire estate, unless there is a will that specifies other arrangements such as certain legacies and gifts or the placement of a trust fund. If all the property, including the marital home, has been gifted elsewhere, the surviving spouse can challenge the will if they feel it to be unfair. If there is no will, then the intestacy rule, set out in the Administration of Estates Act 1925 will apply.

The same now applies to same-sex couples, if their partnership was recognised under the Civil Partnerships Act.

The making of a will may seem unnecessary to younger couples at the time of their wedding, and they may wish to think about their options if they buy property, and again later when perhaps there are children to consider. However, it may be a very important consideration at the time of the wedding for people marrying later in life, or if they are marrying for a second time and there are children from the first marriage. It may also be important to those entering a civil partnership, where again there may be children or other family commitments.

Will arrangements should be made in advance of the wedding, just in case of a tragedy in the early days. It certainly should not be left until some vague future date – that does not arrive. Families can be torn apart by situations where final wishes have remained sketchy or unknown.

When you make a will, you will be asked to nominate an executor, who will ensure that the terms of your will are carried out. In relatively straightforward wills, each spouse or partner can appoint each other to be their executor. Where there are young children or trusts are created, there must be at least two (but no more than four) executors appointed.

A good solicitor who specialises in will-making will be able to provide guidance on how a will can be constructed, taking into account each partner's wishes, and can also give advice on the implications of inheritance tax. Some couples may wish to seek advice together, but a will relates to one person only, so it is quite justifiable to set up appointments individually. Wills are often lodged with a chosen solicitor or at a bank for safekeeping.

Insurance

This may also be the time for couples to review or consider changes to their current life assurance, mortgage or income protection and other forms of insurance cover, naming one another as beneficiaries. Where there is no such cover in place, they may wish to research the kinds of cover appropriate to their new circumstances.

Quick reference 3: Resources

Useful websites

Confetti   www.confetti.co.uk
Wedding Guide UK   www.weddingguide.co.uk

Wedding planners

UK Alliance of Professional
Wedding Planners   www.ukawp.com

Christian tradition

Church of England: www.cofe.anglican.org
Body, Revd A *Growing Together* London: Church House Publishing
Catholic
Marriage Care   www.marriagecare.org.uk
The Methodist Church   www.methodistchurch.org.uk
Baptist Union   www.baptist.org.uk
Religious Society of Friends (The Quakers)   www.quaker.org.uk

Other faiths

Asian wedding planner: Tania Tapel Ltd   www.tania-tapel.com

Civil weddings

England and Wales:
Association of Registration & Celebratory Services   www.arcs.com
Scotland   www.gro-scotland.gov.uk
Northern Ireland   www.groni.uk

Civil partnerships

Stonewall   www.stonewall.org.uk
Pink Weddings   www.pinkweddings.biz

Humanist

British Humanist Association   www.humanism.org.uk

Green weddings:

Green Union   www.greenunion.co.uk
Eco Weddings   www.ecowedding.com
Responsible Travel   www.responsibletravel.com

Weddings abroad

Foreign & Commonwealth Office   www.fco.gov.uk
C'est Deux   www.cestdeux.com

Transport

Perfect Day Cars   www.perfectdaycars.org.uk

Wedding present lists

Wrapit   www.wrapit.co.uk
Alternative Wedding List   www.giveit.co.uk

Passports

Passport Advice Line   0870 521 0410
                                          www.passport.gov.uk

Photography

Society of Wedding & Portrait Photographers   www.swpp.co.uk
Master Photographers Association   www.thempa.com
Institute of British Photographers   www.bipp.com
Julia Boggio Photography   www.juliaboggiophotography.com

Videography

Institute of Videography   www.iov.co.uk
Association of Professional Videomakers   www.apv.org.uk
Wedding & Event Videographers Association   www.weva.com
Bloomsbury Films   www.bloomsburyweddings.com

Toastmasters

National Association of Toastmasters   www.natuk.com

Speechmakers' Training

Oh Crikey!   www.oh-crikey.com

Disc jockeys

National Association of Disc Jockeys   www.nadj.org.uk

Perfect Best Man

George Davidson

All you need to know

- Do you want to make sure you're a great best man?
- Do you want to make the groom glad he chose you?
- Do you need some guidance on your role and responsibilities?

Perfect Best Man is an indispensible guide to every aspect of the best man's role. Covering everything from organising the stag night to making sure the big day runs according to plan, it walks you through exactly what you need to do and gives great advice about getting everything done with the least possible fuss. With checklists to make sure you have it all covered, troubleshooting sections for when things go wrong, and a unique chapter on choosing and organising the ushers, *Perfect Best Man* has everything you need to make sure you rise to the occasion.

BOOKS

Perfect Readings for Weddings

Jonathan Law

All you need to make your special day perfect

- Do you want your wedding to be that little bit more special?
- Do you want to personalise the ceremony by including readings that are just right for you?
- Do you need help tracking down a traditional reading, or finding something more out of the way?

Perfect Readings for Weddings is an anthology of the best poems, prose passages and quotations about love and marriage. Including everything from familiar blessings and verses to more unusual choices, it covers every sort of reading you could wish for. With advice on how to choose readings that complement one another and tips on how to ensure that everything runs smoothly on the day, *Perfect Readings for Weddings* has everything you need to make sure the whole ceremony is both memorable and meaningful.

BOOKS

Perfect Wedding Speeches and Toasts

George Davidson

All you need to give a brilliant speech

- Have you been asked to 'say a few words' on the big day
  and don't quite know how to go about it?
- Do you want easy-to-follow tips on making a speech
  that is both meaningful and memorable?
- Do you want some guidance on how to improve
  your skills as a public speaker?

Perfect Wedding Speeches and Toasts is an invaluable guide to preparing
and delivering unforgettable speeches. Covering everything from
advice on mastering your nerves to tips about how to make a real
impact, it walks you through every aspect of preparing for the big day
and speaking in public. Whether you're the father of the bride, the
bride herself, or the best man, *Perfect Wedding Speeches and Toasts* will
help make sure your speech goes off without a hitch.

BOOKS

Perfect Babies' Names

Rosalind Fergusson

All you need to choose the ideal name

- Do you want help finding the perfect name?
- Are you unsure whether to go for something traditional or something more unusual?
- Do you want to know a bit more about the names you are considering?

Perfect Babies' Names is an essential resource for all parents-to-be. Taking a close look at over 3,000 names, it not only tells you each name's meaning and history, it also tells you which famous people have shared it over the years and how popular – or unpopular – it is now. With tips on how to make a shortlist and advice for avoiding unfortunate nicknames, *Perfect Babies' Names* is the ultimate one-stop guide.

BOOKS

Perfect Pub Quiz

David Pickering

All you need to stage a great quiz

- Who invented the cat-flap?
- Which is the largest island in the world?
- What is tofu made of?

Perfect Pub Quiz is the ideal companion for all general knowledge nuts. Whether you're organising a quiz night in your local or you simply want to get in a bit of practice on tricky subjects, *Perfect Pub Quiz* has all the questions and answers. With topics ranging from the Roman Empire to *Little Britain* and from the Ryder Cup to Alex Rider, this easy-to-use quiz book will tax your brain and provide hours of fun.

BOOKS

Perfect Punctuation

Stephen Curtis

All you need to get it right first time

- Do you find punctuation a bit confusing?
- Are you worried that your written English mate might show you up?
- Do you want a simple way to brush up you skills?

Perfect Punctuation is an invaluble guide to mastering punctuation marks and improving your writing. Covering everything from semi-colons to inverted commas, it gives step-by-step guidance on how to use each mark and how to avoid common mistakes. With helpful examples of correct and incorrect usage and exercises that enable you to practise what you've learned, *Perfect Punctuation* has everything you need to ensure that you never make a mistake again.

BOOKS

Order more titles in the *Perfect* series
from your local bookshop, or have them delivered
direct to your door by Bookpost.

☐ Perfect Answers to Interview Questions	Max Eggert	9781905211722	£7.99
☐ Perfect Babies' Names	Rosalind Fergusson	9781905211661	£5.99
☐ Perfect Calorie Counting	Kate Santon	9781847945181	£6.99
☐ Perfect CV	Max Eggert	9781905211739	£7.99
☐ Perfect Interview	Max Eggert	9781905211746	£7.99
☐ Perfect Numerical Test Results	Joanna Moutafi and Ian Newcombe	9781905211333	£7.99
☐ Perfect Personality Profiles	Helen Baron	9781905211821	£7.99
☐ Perfect Psychometric Test Results	Joanna Moutafi and Ian Newcombe	9781905211678	£7.99
☐ Perfect Pub Quiz	David Pickering	9781905211692	£6.99
☐ Perfect Punctuation	Stephen Curtis	9781905211685	£5.99
☐ Perfect Readings for Weddings	Jonathan Law	9781905211098	£6.99
☐ Perfect Wedding Speeches and Toasts	George Davidson	9781905211777	£5.99
☐ Perfect Written English	Chris West	9781847945037	£5.99

Free post and packing
Overseas customers allow £2 per paperback

Phone: 01624 677237

Post: Random House Books
c/o Bookpost, PO Box 29, Douglas, Isle of Man IM99 1BQ

Fax: 01624 670 923

email: bookshop@enterprise.net

Cheques (payable to Bookpost) and credit cards accepted

Prices and availability subject to change without notice.
Allow 28 days for delivery.
When placing your order, please state if you do not
wish to receive any additional information.

www.rbooks.co.uk